THE POETRY OF POPE'S *DUNCIAD*

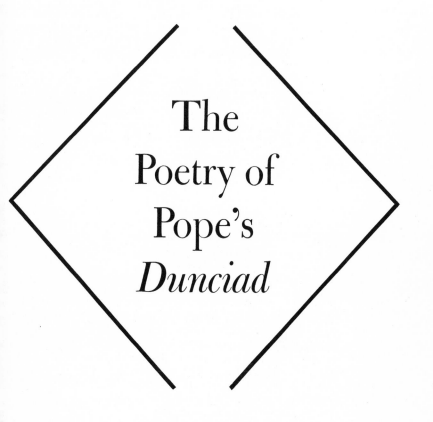

The
Poetry of
Pope's
Dunciad

JOHN E. SITTER

UNIVERSITY OF MINNESOTA PRESS
Minneapolis

Published in the United Kingdom and India by the Oxford University
Press, London and Bombay, and in Canada
by the Copp Clark Publishing Co. Limited, Toronto

Library of Congress Catalog Card Number: 71-167298
ISBN 0-8166-0629-3

Permission to quote from the following volumes
in the *Twickenham Edition of the Poems of Alexander Pope* has been granted by Yale University
Press, New Haven, Conn.: *The Rape of the Lock*,
vol. II, edited by Geoffrey Tillotson; *Epistles to
Several Persons*, vol. III, edited by F. W. Bateson;
Imitations of Horace, vol. IV, edited by John
Butt; *The Dunciad*, vol. V, edited by James R.
Sutherland; *Minor Poems*, vol. VI, edited by Nor-
man Ault and John Butt; and *The Iliad*, vol. VII,
edited by Maynard Mack. Permission to quote
from *The Works of Geoffrey Chaucer*, edited by
Fred N. Robinson, has been granted by Houghton
Mifflin Company, Boston, Mass.

For

< SAMUEL HOLT MONK >

*mentor
and friend*

Contents

THE POETRY OF POPE'S *DUNCIAD*

Introduction

From the beginning Pope knew the *Dunciad* was a difficult poem. He told John Caryll a year after its initial publication that "the poem itself will bear a second reading, or (to express myself more justly and more modestly) will be better borne at the second than first reading. . . ."[1] Pope was not speaking to his longtime friend of the hard surface of topical allusion, although that is the first obstacle confronting a modern reader. Rather, because the poet was a remarkably objective critic as well, he was sufficiently disengaged to recognize, without apology or self-congratulation, the fundamental complexity of his poem. It is a difficult but necessary example to follow.

The *Dunciad* has, of course, borne more than a second reading by admirers of Pope's poetry, and some of those readings have been refined into literary scholarship and criticism. Like his other poems, the *Dunciad* has benefited considerably from the growing attention to Pope's aims and achievement which took root four decades ago with the publication of Austin Warren's *Alexander Pope as Critic and Humanist*. The rest, including the recently completed and definitive *Twickenham Edition of the Poems of Alexander Pope*, is now literary history and need not be repeated here, except to note, specifically, that the *Dunciad* has been paid

3

extensive and intelligent attention by Aubrey L. Williams, whose work, *Pope's "Dunciad": A Study of Its Meaning*, is the only previous work devoted to Pope's longest poem.[2]

Any student of the *Dunciad* is at once indebted to Mr. Williams's study and to James Sutherland's edition (Volume V of the *Twickenham Edition*), and I have tried wherever possible to avoid reiterating information contained in these sources. I have differed at several important points with the interpretative comments of both Mr. Williams and Mr. Sutherland, but it is hardly necessary to say that without their work it would be impossible to deal more freely with other topics. It is to be hoped that one need no longer defend the "morality" or genuine literary merit of satire, including specific satire, and Mr. Williams has, I believe, laid to rest the issue of "libel" in the *Dunciad*: "As Pope's personal enemies enter into his poem they are transformed, but the transformation is possible only by a falsification of their real personalities. The dunces are *not* altogether the same as they were in real life; they have been given a symbolic importance which they lacked in reality. A falsification of personality which, from a strictly moralistic point of view, may be considered reprehensible, can be seen, from a different point of view, as the very source of much of the poem's imaginative power."[3] And so one may proceed.

This study deals primarily with the poetic complexity, the difficulty of the "poem itself," which Pope and other readers have found in the *Dunciad*. The first chapter, which analyzes patterns of imagery and metaphor, is almost exclusively critical. The second chapter considers Pope's poetic practice and irony against the larger background of eighteenth-century ideas of epic and heroic poetry. In the third chapter, which begins with a comparison of the *Dunciad* and the *Temple of Fame*, I attempt to define the iconographic mode and allegorical form of the *Dunciad* and to place the poem in the context of Pope's sometimes unclassical concern for "visionary" poetry.

There remains one problem which I have skirted rather than solved. It is frequently maintained that there are really two dis-

< INTRODUCTION >

tinct *Dunciad*s: the first fully completed by 1729 in three books with Lewis Theobald as its "hero," and the second, with Colley Cibber enthroned, complete in four books and published in 1743. This argument is more problematic than it might first appear, for it presents one of the rare instances of bibliographical history and critical evaluation becoming inextricably intertwined. One can imagine, and certainly envy, the assurance with which Pope's gentle Scriblerus would intercede at this point and cut through the difficulty by proving in his best Scholastic manner that the editions of 1728 and 1729 did not, in fact, exist: "All phantoms!" This study, at any rate, is concerned mainly with the finished *Dunciad* of 1743, the edition which Pope regarded as authoritative, and which certainly is the poem most people read today. But wherever relevant and feasible I have considered the alterations and additions Pope finally incorporated and have tried to show that they are, like most of Pope's revisions, improvements.

< CHAPTER ONE >

"How Farce and Epic
Get a Jumbled Race"
Generic Confusion

That John Dennis, a critic whose judgment Pope continually deprecated, should have established one of the most enduring critical assumptions concerning Pope's most ambitious original work is among the myriad ironies of literary history. When Dennis remarked in 1729 that the *Dunciad* has no real action, that "the Hero of the Piece does nothing at all," he used this assertion to demonstrate that the *Dunciad* is, therefore, an unsuccessful mock epic. Referring to Pope's original invocation, Dennis writes, "Thus *P*. sings Books, and not an Action; and the Author who pretends in an Epick Poem to sing Books instead of singing an Action, is only qualified to sing Ballads. And as Nature has begun to qualify him for that melodious Vocation, by giving him that Face, that Shape, and that Stature . . ."[1] Between digressions (Dennis is scarcely at his best in this pamphlet) he contrasts Pope's poem unfavorably with *Le Lutrin* and *Hudibras*. Later and cooler critics from Joseph Warton to the present, though usually disagreeing strongly with Dennis concerning the *Dunciad*'s merits, have substantially agreed with him on the matters of "action" and mock-heroic poetry.

Among many of the most knowledgeable and ardent admirers of Pope there is a general feeling, consequently, that the *Dunciad*

< GENERIC CONFUSION >

is powerful but sadly uneven: "Considered simply as a mock epic, the *Dunciad* is less successful than *The Rape of the Lock*. . . . The mockery of the epic form is there; but in the *Dunciad* Pope's primary concern is not to write mock epic, but to make use of that form to satirize his enemies. The dunces come first, the *Dunciad* second." Mr. Sutherland's position is not idiosyncratic. Ian Jack concludes that "neither in the version of 1728 nor in that of 1743 is the idiom of the *Dunciad* consistently mock-heroic," and that the poem represents a regrettable regression "right back into the current of vernacular satire." Mr. Williams attempts to counter the charge that the poem lacks action by examining Pope's professed Virgilian analogy and by emphasizing that the "action" is, as Pope makes Scriblerus claim, "the Removal of the Imperial seat of Dulness from the City to the polite world; as that of the *Aeneid* is the Removal of the empire of *Troy* to *Latium*." But despite his careful analysis, he feels the *Dunciad* "may ultimately be classified as only a 'magnificent failure.' " Moreover, Reuben Brower is, I think, justified in arguing that the analogy of the *Aeneid* action and the Lord Mayor's procession gives way after the opening book to a more "prophetic mood."[2]

If the *Dunciad* does suffer in comparison with *The Rape of the Lock* the reason is not that it is an irregular adaptation of Pope's earlier mode; rather, it is that such a comparison is intrinsically invidious. Despite Pope's frequent (and frequently noted) echoes and imitations of epic poets, despite his ironic declarations of epic intent, and despite his obvious, acknowledged debts to Boileau and Garth, the *Dunciad* does not properly belong to the genre which, loose as it may be, embraces *Le Lutrin*, *The Dispensary*—and *The Rape of the Lock*. Certainly Pope is at least partly responsible for the confusion. Not only has he complicated matters by employing many of the devices often found in mock-heroic poems, but he has also, by the consummate success of *The Rape of the Lock*, had more to do with our thinking about mock epic than any other English poet. For the importance of a genre is determined more by the quality than the quantity of its recognizable members. Just as our notions of English tragedy would be vastly different were a handful of plays by Marlowe and Shakespeare not extant at the head of the hundreds of readable plays subsumed under that genre, and just as our vague ideas of what English epic should do would be even more diffuse were there no *Paradise Lost* to give them focus, so it is unlikely that we could talk with much assurance about the "mock epic" were it not for the conspicuous presence of *The Rape of the Lock*.

Whatever the effect of *The Rape of the Lock* on our critical predispositions, the *Dunciad* has little in common with it at bottom other than the wide range of allusion which, as Mr. Brower has eloquently argued, is a vital element in all of Pope's poetry. The *Dunciad* has much more complex principles of organization than either *The Rape of the Lock* or that poem's great precursors, and it consequently has a more complex structure. This structure, as I will attempt to demonstrate later, derives from a variety of historical origins, of which the mock-heroic poem is only one, and, in fact, a relatively minor one: looming much larger are the so-called progress piece and the dream-vision. Both of these genres—one a primarily post-Renaissance phenomenon, the other primarily pre-Renaissance—are much more central to the lifelong poetic ideas and ideals of Pope than has been commonly recognized. In his taste, at least, Pope was profoundly catholic, and these two modes of poetry inform the early *Dunciad* more than does the mock-heroic mode; by 1743 they are explored and extended even further.

These are, however, complicated and complicating elements which must be discussed separately. At this point it may be useful to consider that, whatever the historical influences on the composition of the *Dunciad*, the result is something closer to "anti-epic" than to mock epic. I will attempt to justify the particular use of "anti-epic" later, but, for the moment, it can be employed merely descriptively to accommodate differences in "plot" and tone which have long been recognized between the *Dunciad* on the one hand and *Le Lutrin*, *The Dispensary*, and *The Rape of the Lock* on the other.

In both respects the differences are fundamental. The *Dunciad*'s

< GENERIC CONFUSION >

tone differs mainly by sustaining a higher level of seriousness. This is not to deny, certainly, that the mock epics may and do have complex ethical implications; nor is it to deny, conversely, that the *Dunciad* is playful and humorous as well as ironic, or even (as Mr. Sutherland remarks) that Pope "rarely wrote anything in such high spirits as the *Dunciad* of 1728–9."[3] The issues at stake are simply larger and more ponderous. One need not invoke Arnoldian criteria of "high seriousness" to realize that we might comfortably call the poems of Boileau, Garth, and the young Pope jeux d'esprit (regardless of what we might think of their worth), but to apply such a phrase to the *Dunciad,* even in its original form, would be grotesque. And because the issues are more essential, the poem's characters assume a perverse importance. Unlike the actors in a mock epic, they are not ultimately guilty of mere inflated pettiness; they are guilty of being significant, and their behavior is not only ludicrous but crucial.[4]

The difference in action or "plot" has been mentioned. In the *Dunciad* there is little that can be called action in the conventional sense: there is an abundance of activity, but anything larger or more unified must be abstracted from that. In the mock epics under discussion the action depicted is petty, but in each case it is an action and one which has been completed in the past. The subject of the *Dunciad,* however, is a state of being (not an action) existing in the present and future (rather than concluded in the past), and, inevitably, this difference has its effect on form.

It is impossible to be certain just how aware Pope was of transmuting new material into a new form. One cannot know, for example, if he was fully conscious that his Scriblerian declaration, with its analysis of the poem in terms of mock epic, is at least a pink herring. But with a poet as alive to poetic tradition and genres as Pope—in this respect perhaps the most self-conscious poet between Milton and Eliot—we are probably safe in assuming considerable awareness. Ian Jack finds fault with Pope because in the *Dunciad* he "turned his back" on mock-heroic satire.[5] If that is an accurate description, one might imagine that Pope felt

9

he had already "twich't his Mantle blue" before he turned toward new pastures. But the problem here, in a preliminary exploration of the *Dunciad* itself, is not to determine precisely what Pope knew of his poetry in 1728 or even in 1743, but rather to approach the *Dunciad* as nearly as possible in the spirit its author "writ." This means, if not classifying it exactly, at least shunning the "high Priori Road" and the misleading classification of mock epic. It may be that the loose concept of anti-epic, because it carries no automatic demands, will allow a more empirical approach and permit contact with more points of Pope's satire, which is to say—with Pope's poetry.

1.

It is clear that some of these same issues, the problems and provinces of literary kinds, are an important concern of the *Dunciad* and work their way into the fabric of the poem itself. Generic blurring immediately becomes both part and emblem of a parade of fundamental anarchy. Reviewing her own "wild creation" the goddess Dulness stations herself at the "Cave of Poverty and Poetry," where

> . . . motley Images her fancy strike,
> Figures ill pair'd, and Similes unlike.
> She sees a Mob of Metaphors advance,
> Pleas'd with the madness of the mazy dance:
> How Tragedy and Comedy embrace;
> How Farce and Epic get a jumbled race;
> How Time himself stands still at her command,
> Realms shift their place, and Ocean turns to land.
>
> (B, i, 65–72) [6]

Personification seems almost too somber a word to describe Pope's technique here: the literary quantities are animated into the puppetlike rapidity of "the madness of the mazy dance" with great comic skill. The remainder of the paragraph turns upon writers who will never understand the need of being versed in natural things:

< GENERIC CONFUSION >

Here gay Description Ægypt glads with show'rs,
Or gives to Zembla fruits, to Barca flow'rs;
Glitt'ring with ice here hoary hills are seen,
There painted vallies of eternal green,
In cold December fragrant chaplets blow,
And heavy harvests nod beneath the snow.

(B, i, 73–78)

Pope is having great fun matching sound to sense, or to what seems to be the sense; the first couplet marches in brisk display, and the next two languish in lushness. But beneath the amusement there is a serious premonition of the consequences of confusion. Ostensibly Pope has merely shifted the targets of his satire, from bathetic drama, for example, to synthetic pastoral, but the shift is actually more elemental. In a dozen lines Pope manages to suggest imagistically that violations of artistic decorum are really violations of Nature, that they are fundamentally unnatural. (One might recapture some of that adjective's emotive force, blunted even for readers of Augustan literature, if he imagines it as one of E. E. Cummings's anti-words, derived from "un-Nature.") If tragedy embraces comedy, or farce joins forces with epic, the result is not rightful fertility but prodigious promiscuity. If metaphors, which should in their construction call into employment the delicate combination of discrimination and judgment, exist instead in a state of mob rule, their very presence suggests the precedence of passion and whim over reason and nature. And if the most basic laws of nature are sacrificed for the convenience of pseudo-art and ignorance, then nature itself is threatened. For, in a curious way, the philosophical principle underlying this passage is close to Wilde's aphorism that "nature imitates art": human industry and knowledge are what establish, reveal, and preserve the natural order.

This would seem too solemn a reading of these lines were it not for the fact that they are linked by metaphorical suggestion to other passages in Book I which imply other forms of natural confusion and shapelessness. Images particularly of grotesque and incongruous birth repeatedly occur early in the *Dunciad*. The narrative begins retrospectively, "E'er Pallas issu'd from the Thund'rer's head," with the account of the birth of Dulness out of Chaos and Night:

> Fate in their dotage this fair Ideot gave,
> Gross as her sire, and as her mother grave,
> Laborious, heavy, busy, bold, and blind,
> She rul'd, in native Anarchy, the mind.
>
> (B, i, 13–16)

This is followed by the promise of another generation to come:

> . . . behold her mighty wings out-spread
> To hatch a new Saturnian age of Lead.
>
> (B, i, 27–28)

In his revision of this book Pope exploited these passages by setting his scene in descriptive terms that would echo the confused productivity of those primal parents and of Dulness herself. Just as he had suggested the undesirable, inherited attributes of Dulness through jarring alliteration—"busy, bold, and blind"— so he described in 1743 the location near Bedlam,

> Where o'er the gates, by his fam'd father's hand
> Great Cibber's brazen, brainless brothers stand.
>
> (B, i, 31–32)

Colley Cibber's "brothers" are two statues of lunatics produced by his father, a sculptor of some employ if not note. The joke is a good one, but it is more than a passing shot, for the stillborn statues are the third instance so early in the poem of unnatural and symptomatic procreation.

With a very slight revision, too, the final version of the Cave of Poverty and Poetry, which Dulness visits as her special province, becomes a kind of monstrous womb:

> Hence Bards, like Proteus long in vain ty'd down,
> Escape in Monsters, and amaze the town.
> Hence Miscellanies spring, the weekly boast
> Of Curl's chaste press, and Lintot's rubric post:
> Hence hymning Tyburn's elegiac lines,
> Hence Journals, Medleys, Merc'ries, Magazines:

< GENERIC CONFUSION >

> Sepulchral Lyes, our holy walls to grace,
> And New-year Odes, and all the Grub-street race.
>
> (B, i, 37–44)

The source of such ill-formed productions is carefully molded by
Pope into an imagistic structure primitive and strong enough to
support the specific satire built upon it. The initial repetition of
"Hence . . ." reinforces the effect of verbs like "escape" and
"spring," and the "Miscellanies," the product of a kind of abstract
miscegenation, are here the almost physical offspring of a "press"
and "post." And from the Cave comes a whole new "race." A
similar process operates in Pope's description of the inside of
the Cave:

> Here she beholds the Chaos dark and deep,
> Where nameless Somethings in their causes sleep,
> 'Till genial Jacob, or a warm Third day,
> Call forth each mass, a Poem, or a Play:
> How hints, like spawn, scarce quick in embryo lie,
> How new-born nonsense first is taught to cry,
> Maggots half-form'd in rhyme exactly meet,
> And learn to crawl upon poetic feet.
>
> (B, i, 55–62)

Much earlier in his career Pope had used amorphous existence
as the basis for imagistic denigration. In the *Essay on Criticism*
he referred to writers who are neither critics nor poets as "half-
form'd Insects on the Banks of *Nile*," and named them as best
he could—

> Unfinish'd Things, one knows not what to call,
> Their Generation's so equivocal.
>
> (*EOC*, I, 41–43)

But in the *Dunciad* he turns a casual epithet into an actual principle of metaphorical organization. The "Maggots half-form'd"
and the "nameless Somethings" become part of a uterine context
enclosing "embryo" and "new-born nonsense" as well.[7]

After Dulness observes the jumbled race begotten by farce,
epic, and other "figures ill pair'd," she reflects upon the day's
activities:

13

> Much to the mindful Queen the feast recalls
> What City Swans once sung within the walls;
> Much she revolves their arts, their ancient praise,
> And sure succession down from Heywood's days.
> She saw, with joy, the line immortal run,
> Each sire imprest and glaring in his son:
> So watchful Bruin forms, with plastic care,
> Each growing lump, and brings it to a Bear.
> She saw old Pryn in restless Daniel shine,
> And Eusden eke out Blackmore's endless line.
>
> (B, i, 95–104)

The final pun on "line" epitomizes the relation, both jocular and profound, which Pope establishes in the first book between subliterary creation and distorted, subhuman procreation. The lines on Bruin, which could easily fit into a pastoral description, here equate the "endless" and "immortal" line of dunces with an undifferentiated "lump," and thus with the earlier images of monsters, embryos, and maggots. The sense of the lines depends on the folk theory that bears lick their offspring into shape after birth, and it may be more than incidental that the lines recall similar metaphors from Shakespeare and Donne. In *3 Henry VI* Richard speaks of his misshapen back,

> Where sits deformity to mock my body;
> To shape my legs of an unequal size;
> To disproportion me in every part,
> Like to a chaos, or an unlick'd bear-whelp,
> That carries no impression like the dam.

And in "Elegy XVIII" Donne adapts the metaphor to describe "Loves Progress":

> Love is a bear-whelp born, if we o're lick
> Our love, and force it new strange shapes to take,
> We erre, and of a lump a monster make.
>
> (4–6)

Whether or not Pope had either Shakespeare (whom he had recently edited) or Donne in mind, his own metaphor serves a somewhat similar function—suggesting that a dunce is "like to

< GENERIC CONFUSION >

a chaos" or a "monster"—even though the trouble with the dunces and the dunces' writings is that they have been brought to resemble their ursine "parents" entirely too closely. With "plastic care" the children of Dulness beget and nurture an "endless line" of their own chaotic kind.

The association which has been established between literary and physical procreation is strengthened in the following description of Cibber. Both Cibber's own birth and his capacity for giving birth figure in this characterization of the laureate:

> In each she marks her Image full exprest,
> But chief in BAYS's monster-breeding breast;
> Bays, form'd by nature Stage and Town to bless,
> And act, and be, a Coxcomb with success.
>
> (B, i, 107–110)

As Pope describes Cibber at work the images of birth become more graphic. We see him after the "thin Third day" of his latest theatrical venture trying to give birth to another literary production:

> Round him much Embryo, much Abortion lay,
> Much future Ode, and abdicated Play.
>
> (B, i, 121–122)

This couplet is among those Pope added to this section when he revised it in 1743. The original passage, which simply described the despairing Theobald in the midst of the "learned lumber" (A, i, 116) of his library, was adequate to characterize a hapless hack, but it was not particularly original. An anonymous satirist, for example, had represented Sir Richard Blackmore in a similar situation, and with much the same effect, as early as 1721:

> Here, in a loathsome Cave, emcompassed round
> With Reams of Verse, the moody Quack he found.

But in revising the description Pope turned what was virtually a satiric cliché into an integral part of his poem's metaphorical framework.[8] The same is true of another couplet which Pope added to summarize Cibber's literary work:

15

> All that on Folly Frenzy could beget,
> Fruits of dull Heat, and Sooterkins of Wit.
>
> (B, i, 125–126)

Pope has improved in the second line upon Dryden's "Kilderkin of wit" (one of the epithets ladled upon Shadwell) by substituting the folk term for a mouselike animal supposedly born of a human mother. Cibber is, in other words, laboring over a misconception. The result is that we again witness blatant and jocose denigration moving on the same "poetic feet" with a more subtle and refined system of imagistic evocation. Cibber's literary brothers are lumpish bear cubs, his finished works are "sooterkins," and his half-finished productions are stillborn embryos: we begin to realize that the world of dull writing is abortive as well as absurd, chaotic as well as comic.

Pope turns even a forced revision into a strategic reminder of grotesque procreation. When he described Theobald setting fire to his works, Pope had written, "And last, a little Ajax tips the spire" (A, i, 142). This reference to a duodecimo edition of Sophocles obviously would not do for laureate Cibber. In its final form the line becomes "A twisted Birth-day Ode completes the spire" (B, i, 162). And this revision is echoed later when the "sparkling brand" with which Theobald had ignited the pyre turns, in Cibber's hands, into a "Birth-day brand" (A, i, 203; B, i, 245).

2.

Pope's Cibber becomes, little by little, a kind of archetype of literary confusion growing inevitably into a more comprehensive natural confusion. Reviewing his career, the laureate and dramatist who had recently written an "Apology"[9] for his life now "apologizes" for *The Careless Husband*, the one play of Cibber's which Pope considered competent:

> Some Dæmon stole my pen (forgive th' offence)
> And once betray'd me into common sense:
> Else all my Prose and Verse were much the same;

< GENERIC CONFUSION >

> This, prose on stilts; that, poetry fall'n lame.
> Did on the stage my Fops appear confin'd?
> My Life gave ampler lessons to mankind.
> Did the dead Letter unsuccessful prove?
> The brisk Example never fail'd to move.
>
> (B, i, 187–194)

Cibber's entire energies, according to this new Apology, have been directed toward violating, blurring, and destroying important distinctions. To write poetry which is only elevated prose ("on stilts") or prose which is merely halting fustian ("poetry fall'n lame") is directly analogous to the confusion of having "Realms shift their place." To misappropriate the respective roles of good stagecraft (Cibber's "dead Letter") and good living (the "brisk Example") is equivalent to the artistic and natural disorder inaugurated when "Ocean turns to land." The ideal author for Pope, particularly by 1743 when these lines were included, would write with fire and force but live in tranquillity and benevolence; Cibber's "Life," however, had proved (both in its literary and actual versions) to be his best performance in the role of pert coxcomb.

It is because of his innate aptitude for wrongheaded creativity that Pope's Cibber can be said to bear the "Image" of Dulness so clearly in his "monster-breeding breast," for such confused creation is the precise province of Dulness herself. Cibber attends her to "her sacred Dome" where

> . . . to her Chosen all her works she shews;
> Prose swell'd to verse, verse loit'ring into prose:
> How random thoughts now meaning chance to find,
> Now leave all memory of sense behind:
> How Prologues into Prefaces decay,
> And these to Notes are fritter'd quite away.
>
> (B, i, 273–278)

The description could serve for one of Cibber's own workshops, replete with "embryo" and "abortion."

The Dome of Dulness is itself one of the finest inventions of Pope's imagination. In addition to providing the poet with some

17

nice opportunities for mock-philosophical argument, it also furnishes the first book with the widest possible metaphorical range. For the Dome functions as an ontological objectification of all that Pope's Cibber has come to represent. Not only is it a place where monstrosities are on exhibit, but it is also a confused and indeterminate realm by its very nature; or, rather, it is the preternatural equivalent of Cibber's neither-this-nor-that nature. Good and evil traditionally find their theological completion in a heaven and a hell; but for the representatives of insistent nothingness, a vague limbo will serve justly as a spiritual home, and that is what the Dome of Dulness provides.

Pope does not bring us to this point unprepared. We have seen that Cibber is not, directly, an agent of good or evil but rather a catalyst for dissolution, capable of dissolving natural distinctions in society as well as in art:

> This brazen Brightness, to the 'Squire so dear;
> This polish'd Hardness, that reflects the Peer;
> This arch Absurd, that wit and fool delights;
> This Mess, toss'd up of Hockley-hole and White's;
> Where Dukes and Butchers join to wreathe my crown,
> At once the Bear and Fiddle of the town.

> (B, i, 219–224)

And we have seen him as an anxious parent wishing a similar fate for his "progeny," one which is not connected, directly, with good or evil, success or failure:

> "O born in sin, and forth in folly brought!
> Works damn'd, or to be damn'd! (your father's fault)
> Go, purify'd by flames ascend the sky,
> My better and more christian progeny!
> Unstain'd, untouch'd, and yet in maiden sheets;
> While all your smutty sisters walk the streets.
> Ye shall not beg, like gratis-given Bland,
> Sent with a Pass, and vagrant thro' the land;
> Not sail, with Ward, to Ape-and-monkey climes,
> Where vile Mundungus trucks for viler rhymes;
> Not sulphur-tipt, emblaze an Ale-house fire;
> Not wrap up Oranges, to pelt your sire!

< GENERIC CONFUSION >

O! pass more innocent, in infant state,
To the mild Limbo of our Father Tate:
Or peaceably forgot, at once be blest
In Shadwell's bosom with eternal Rest!
Soon to that mass of Nonsense to return,
Where things destroy'd are swept to things unborn."

(B, i, 225–242)

We might also linger over these lines because they afford us a happy opportunity to reconstruct the evolution of a poetic concept. Pope had begun in 1728 with a much shorter passage, a six-line apostrophe in which Theobald had wished to preserve his works from some of the inglorious fates that Cibber mentions:

"Adieu my children! better thus expire
Unstall'd, unsold; thus glorious mount in fire
Fair without spot; than greas'd by grocer's hands,
Or shipp'd with Ward to ape and monkey lands,
Or wafting ginger, round the streets to go,
And visit alehouse where ye first did grow."

(A, i, 197–202)

The transformation of Theobald's brief reflection into Cibber's full-fledged conceit—in which the possibilities of the equation of literary and actual "children" are drawn out in a manner at once more comic and ominous—illustrates how Pope was able to exploit his material by constantly synthesizing it, and in this case three distinct elements have gone into the synthesis. First, with the elevation of Cibber, Pope allowed his imagination to dwell freely on the laureate's own ludicrous comparison of his actual and theatrical "children."[10] Hence the line "My better and more christian progeny!" This in turn seems to have given Pope room to turn the original suggestion for the passage—Dryden's banishment of Shadwell to "some peaceful province in acrostic land"— into the "mild Limbo" which might well house a Cibber and all his progeny in "eternal Rest." The characterization is already much deeper, since Pope's Cibber, instinctively confused as he is, now longs for an abode of confusion exempt from the demands of good or bad writing—or of good or bad.

19

Poetry of Pope's *Dunciad*

Our third consideration has to do with Pope's brilliant closing couplet:

> Soon to that mass of Nonsense to return,
> Where things destroy'd are swept to things unborn.

Alluding to a very similar (and very solemn) couplet in a poem of Rochester's, Pope was able to round off this new conceit of "innocent" progeny and Limbo.[11] We are reminded that the "things unborn" and the "things destroy'd," which together make up the massy Nonsense of duncery, are also part of that mindless confusion which is abortive and annihilating.

The Limbo conceit dominating Cibber's long speech is so finely controlled and so ominously evocative that we momentarily forget the speaker. But Pope is content to let the suggestion of universal destruction remain only a suggestion until later in the poem, and he quickly sweeps us along with Cibber to the Dome of Dulness. It is clear that Cibber's prayer has been answered, for the Dome is a literary Limbo. After exhibiting several artistic monstrosities, Dulness shows Cibber

> How Index-learning turns no student pale,
> Yet holds the eel of science by the tail:
> How, with less reading than makes felons scape,
> Less human genius than God gives an ape,
> Small thanks to France, and none to Rome or Greece,
> A past, vamp'd, future, old, reviv'd, new piece,
> 'Twixt Plautus, Fletcher, Shakespear, and Corneille,
> Can make a Cibber, Tibbald, or Ozell.
>
> (B, i, 279–286)

If Pope's criticism were merely literary, merely one-dimensional, the Dome of Dulness would be no more than a museum; instead, it is a matrix. This Limbo where no distinction is made between a Corneille and an Ozell, between human genius and an ape, is the spiritual womb and tomb of the worldly Cave of Poverty and Poetry "where nameless Somethings in their causes sleep."[12]

The Dome also has a very important function in the *Dunciad* as a whole, for it serves as an imagistic connection between the

< GENERIC CONFUSION >

Cave of the opening section and the underworld dominating Book III. The description of the "Elysian Shade" which Cibber visits in the third book is in part a comic version of Virgil's underworld in Book VI of the *Aeneid*, and Pope emphasizes the parallels:

> Here, in a dusky vale where Lethe rolls,
> Old Bavius sits, to dip poetic souls,
> And blunt the sense, and fit it for a skull
> Of solid proof, impenetrably dull.
>   (B, iii, 23–26)

But the description begins to resonate with another sort of insistence as well:

> Instant, when dipt, away they wing their flight,
> Where Brown and Mears unbar the gates of Light,
> Demand new bodies, and in Calf's array,
> Rush to the world, impatient for the day.
> Millions and millions on these banks he views,
> Thick as the stars of night, or morning dews,
> As thick as bees o'er vernal blossoms fly,
> As thick as eggs at Ward in Pillory.
>   (B, iii, 27–34)

Virgil is still in the background, of course, but Pope, in playing freely over Dryden's rather loose rendering of the meeting of Aeneas and Anchises,[13] moves further away from the Elysian Shade and closer to a realm of fecundity like Spenser's Garden of Adonis. As in the descriptions of the Cave of Poverty and Poetry and the Dome of Dulness, Pope's emphasis is on the birth-giving quality of these poetic correlatives for limbo, the place of equivocal generations. In *The Faerie Queene* the Garden of Adonis is dependent at least partly upon classical myth and poetry, but one sees most clearly in Spenser's characterization the element of comically confused energy which Pope could turn to his own use in the *Dunciad*. The porter of Spenser's Garden has a function similar to that of Bavius, Brown, and Mears, and his perspective is similar to that granted the dreaming Cibber. Of the porter Spenser says,

21

> He letteth in, he letteth out to wend
> All that to come into the world desire:
> A thousand thousand naked babes attend
> About him day and night, which doe require
> That he with fleshly weeds would them attire:
> Such as him list, such as eternal fate
> Ordained hath, he clothes with sinfull mire,
> And sendeth forth to live in mortall state,
> Till they agayn returne backe by the hinder gate.
>
> (III, vi, 32)

Whether Pope had Spenser in mind at this point is not paramount. I suspect that he did, since Pope had more "use" for the Spenserian tradition than is normally supposed; but here he may well have been recalling Plato, Lucretius, or Ovid.[14]

It is clear, however, that the profound inversions informing the descriptions of these three realms (the Cave of Poverty and Poetry, Dome of Dulness, and underworld), which gradually coalesce as the limbo of duncery, are not primarily parodic imitations of the *Iliad* or *Aeneid*, but general echoes of pagan allegories of fecundity. Though specific imitation is certainly present and certainly funny, Pope knows it is not enough to hold the poetry together. As is so often the case in the *Dunciad*, Pope uses mock-heroic language, analogy, or situation as one referent—to a knowledgeable reader the most obvious referent—of his satire. But while flashes of imitation glitter on the brilliant surface, patterns of imagery like those we have noticed often move more ponderously. Long after we have stopped smiling at the incongruous rhetoric, the poetic incongruity of massive, ominous fertility still stirs our less conscious responses. Even within the first book of the *Dunciad* Pope manages to bring primarily literary criticisms—criticisms of bad writers and bad writing—to a level of mythic significance, and he does so through the systematic use of images of a grotesque, misshapen, and absurd Genesis which has Dulness, the "Mighty Mother," as its Prime Mover.

In this heavy atmosphere of embryo, abortion, and all the other "sooterkins" of dull wit, Pope is able to range back and forth between the most metaphysical and most grossly physical exten-

< GENERIC CONFUSION >

sions of the "mass of Nonsense" which includes all the progeny of Dulness, both the persons and productions of the dunces. It is this essential imagistic logic, embracing all varieties of confusion and gradually equating them, that provides much of the "point" of Pope's humor at every level. In Book II physical images of massy confusion assume an important role.

3.

For various reasons, the second book of the *Dunciad* seems to make many readers uneasy. Mr. Jack, for example, finds the language too near the idiom of "burlesque," and Mr. Brower, remarking upon the general success of Pope's revision in Book I, argues that "no one can speak so cheerfully of Book II, the 'Games' of the authors, which is a piece of deliberate Scriblerian burlesque." I, for one, must confess to approaching Book II with considerable cheerfulness and to thinking that it succeeds on a higher plane than either of these critics would grant. Mr. Brower charges that, "unlike Pope's subtler parodies," Book II "hardly gives us a truly heroic measure of the little world of the poem, or a sense of a more complex evaluation of any sort."[15] This is a serious criticism, but I think it will become apparent that it ignores the fact that Pope's "complex evaluation" in the second book—as elsewhere—rests more upon complex imagery than upon mock-heroic restraint, and that the scanty narrative of Book II is supported by the coherence and relevance of Pope's imagistic method.

Another complaint, or perhaps the same complaint in different garb, concerns the prominence of scatology in the second book. But it need not be reargued here that scatology has an essential function in much of the best English satire, and it is possible to appreciate particularly Pope's use of scatology in the *Dunciad* when one hears him describing his England five years before the poem's first publication. In 1723 Pope urged the Earl of Peter-borow to stay in England for the sake of his friends: "Others indeed of this nation can spare you, for you have dwelt among us here but like a sort of Noah, preaching Sense & Honour many

years, to a Generation who are doomd to be swallowd up &
drownd in their own Dulness & Dirtiness."[16] One catches the note
of playfully hyperbolic flattery common in much of Pope's correspondence, but the phrasing also reminds one how vivid the
connection between mindlessness and mire was for Pope.

By 1728 Pope does not seem to have changed his mind about
the generation around him. Mire of one sort or another oozes its
way through most of Book II. The first striking instance is the
footrace between booksellers Lintot and Curll. Pope has the
latter winning that contest until

> Full in the middle way there stood a lake,
> Which Curl's Corinna chanc'd that morn to make:
> (Such was her wont, at early dawn to drop
> Her evening cates before his neighbour's shop,)
> Here fortun'd Curl to slide; loud shout the band,
> And Bernard! Bernard! rings thro' all the Strand.
> Obscene with filth the miscreant lies bewray'd,
> Fal'n in the plash his wickedness had laid.
>
> (B, ii, 69–76) [17]

Pope's ambiguity in the last line seems designed to suggest that
Curll's "wickedness" is both his pseudonymous assistant and his
own preconceived plot to trip Lintot; in either case it is made
clear that the "plash" is Curll's doing rather than Pope's. After
this mishap, "Then first . . . the caitiff Vaticide conceiv'd a
prayer," and Jove grants him his dubious success:

> Renew'd by ordure's sympathetic force,
> As oil'd with magic juices for the course,
> Vig'rous he rises; from th' effluvia strong
> Imbibes new life, and scours and stinks along;
> Re-passes Lintot, vindicates the race,
> Nor heeds the brown dishonours of his face.
>
> (B, ii, 103–108)

Obviously part of Pope's fun is to get his contestants as dirty as
possible while still keeping the heroic funeral games of Homer
and Virgil in the visible background. But as the games instituted
by Dulness proceed, it also becomes apparent that Pope is using

< GENERIC CONFUSION >

the mire of his setting for a more subtle purpose than mere mud-slinging. Whereas in the *Aeneid*, for example, games were conducted first on the water and then on the land, in the *Dunciad* even that distinction becomes blurred. The footrace is run in mire and the diving match which follows is held in mire barely covered with water. When the dunces have moved past Bridewell they come

> To where Fleet-ditch with disemboguing streams
> Rolls the large tribute of dead dogs to Thames,
> The King of dykes! than whom no sluice of mud
> With deeper sable blots the silver flood.
> "Here strip, my children! here at once leap in,
> Here prove who best can dash thro' thick and thin,
> And who the most in love of dirt excel,
> Or dark dexterity of groping well."
> (B, ii, 271–278)

The landscape of duncical exercise is an utterly undifferentiated one, one where in miniature "Ocean turns to land" and land to ocean. As a consequence of Pope's careful stage setting the mud comes to represent not only befoulment but also the lowest forms of impermanence and confusion:

> Next plung'd a feeble, but a desp'rate pack,
> With each a sickly brother at his back:
> Sons of a Day! just buoyant on the flood,
> Then number'd with the puppies in the mud.
> Ask ye their names? I could as soon disclose
> The names of these blind puppies as of those.
> . . . .
> And Monumental Brass this record bears,
> "These are,—ah no! these were, the Gazetteers!"
> (B, ii, 305–310; 313–314)

These "Sons of a Day," like the "half-form'd Insects on the Banks of *Nile*" who appeared in the *Essay on Criticism,* are perfectly at home in mud: their existence can be transferred to something as stable as metal only with considerable—ah! readjustment.

It is not so much because of their connotation as because of

25

their physical composition and consistency that slime and excrement provide the proper media for the dunces' confused activity.
For example, Pope dramatizes the dunces' compromised situa-
tions at several points by choosing verbs which suggest only the
vaguest sort of motion across the undifferentiated "field of glory."
Thus in the previously quoted narrative of Curll's misfortune the
reader sees Curll lying in excrement and then comes to the lines

> Vig'rous he *rises*; from th' effluvia strong
> *Imbibes* new life, and *scours* and *stinks* along;
> *Re-passes* Lintot, *vindicates* the race,
> Nor heeds the brown dishonours of his face.

The reader *knows* that Curll has won the race (and rather inglor-
iously), but no description of a well-defined action has been
offered. Verbs like *scour, stink,* and *vindicate* may imply expended
energy but they also imply that it has been expended diffusely. It
is the flailing, confused motion depicted in Pope's fine adaptation
of Milton:

> As when a dab-chick waddles thro' the copse
> On feet and wings, and flies, and wades, and hops;
> So lab'ring on, with shoulders, hands, and head,
> Wide as a wind-mill all his figures spread,
> With arms expanded Bernard rows his state,
> And left-legg'd Jacob seems to emulate.
>
> (B, ii, 63–68) [18]

Pope makes his actors more ridiculous by allowing the reader to
visualize them all too clearly but obscuring their precise actions
in layers of language. This is not simply the effect of "verbal dis-
tancing," which Mr. Williams points to as the result of elegant
diction,[19] for there is nothing particularly elegant about most of
these verbs. Moreover, Pope contrives to clog the actions with
mystery (to literally thicken the plot as it were) by carefully failing
to name the expected physical details. With all the bustle of the
"dab-chick" passage above, for instance, there is no mention of
Lintot moving his *legs*.

Pope claimed that by avoiding obscene diction "our author . . .

< GENERIC CONFUSION >

tosses about his Dung with an air of Majesty."[20] In a sense his claim is justified, and much of the enjoyment of Book II derives from the "shock of recognition" which comes when the reader realizes it is indeed dung that is being tossed. And yet there are numerous points at which Pope's periphrasis is laden with innuendo even less delicate than the subject matter. When he describes the unvictorious urinator with the lines,

> First Osborne lean'd against his letter'd post;
> It rose, and labour'd to a curve at most,
>
> (B, ii, 171–172)

there is a strong suggestion, due to the ambiguous "it," of abiding impotence as well as occasional insufficiency. And, of course, the infamous lines describing Curll's attempt,

> Thro' half the heav'ns he pours th' exalted urn;
> His rapid waters in their passage burn,
>
> (B, ii, 183–184)

suggest the conquest of disease as well as the triumph of "happy Impudence." But these lines (which in *their* passages burn) are memorable not because they are slyly scandalous but because they are surprisingly static. In each instance Pope has caught the action to such a degree that it is transformed into an arrested gesture; the description becomes statuesque as action is transformed into habit and characteristic expression.

Another way in which Pope exploits his sordid setting as an emblem of pervasive confusion is by having that setting elicit contradictory activity from the dunces. So when Oldmixon prepared to dive into Fleet Ditch, he

> . . . climb'd a stranded lighter's height,
> Shot to the black abyss, and plung'd down-right.
>
> (B, ii, 287–288)

And naturally,

> The Senior's judgment all the crowd admire,
> Who but to sink the deeper, rose the higher.
>
> (B, ii, 289–290)

27

The same sort of perverse logic—normally self-contradictory but inevitable in the world of Book II—surrounds the dive of Arnall as

> . . . with a weight of skull,
> Furious he dives, precipitately dull.
> Whirlpools and storms his circling arms invest,
> With all the might of gravitation blest.
> No crab more active in the dirty dance,
> Downward to climb, and backward to advance.
>
> (B, ii, 315–320)

Thus, even when the movement is relatively apparent, one kind of motion is canceled out by its negative in the muddy landscape. The "dirty dance" which Pope's dunces execute becomes emblematic of obvious motion or activity without significant action.

Pope could have demeaned the dunces in conventional mock-heroic fashion by having them simply perform ludicrous versions of heroic contests, without the use of scatological material. But that is not his point, and it is a mistake to regard the filth as something piled on pinioned victims for good measure. The use of all the "majesty of Mud" is essential to the second book not as a means of underscoring mock-heroic action, but rather as a medium in which *anti*-action can move and have its being. And activity such as this, activity incapable of coming to anything other than grotesque and undifferentiated fruition, is not only ludicrous, but also potentially "uncreating."

Pope further extends the visual reality of underlying confusion through the facial expressions of his dunces. Usually these expressions are representative of more than simple mockery. Although there is, for example, facile ridicule in merely using the adjective "Parnassian" to describe Cibber's face, the description quickly unfolds into a more subtle representation of indiscriminateness where the medium is both message and mission.

> . . . The proud Parnassian sneer,
> The conscious simper, and the jealous leer,
> Mix on his look: All eyes direct their rays
> On him, and crowds turn Coxcombs as they gaze.
>
> (B, ii, 5–8)

< GENERIC CONFUSION >

Passages like this convince one that Pope gained much more than he lost by replacing Theobald with Cibber. The earlier version, concluding with "and crowds grow *foolish* as they gaze," was intended to convey exactly the same ideas: that typical duncery wears a remarkably undistinguished expression, and, more importantly, that the vague visage of an arch-dunce has the power of blurring individual distinctions among its audience. Either Theobald or Cibber is capable of bringing "to one dead level ev'ry mind," as Pope would phrase it in Book IV. But the superiority here of the "Cibberian forehead" lies in the fact that Cibber's was the public face of a theatrical figure who excelled famously as a coxcomb; the claim is plausible, in other words, that his face (like the faces of his modern television and cinema counterparts) had much to do with "leveling" the aspirations of his more susceptible viewers.

This same emblematic nonexpression appears on the face of Eliza Haywood, the "Juno of majestic size, With cow-like udders, and with ox-like eyes," whom Curll leads away "pleas'd" and "soft-smiling" (B, i, 164-5, 188). And it appears again in the reflected vapidity of the patron who "grins, and looks broad nonsense with a stare" as eager dedicators vie for his attention:

Now gentle touches wanton o'er his face,
He struts Adonis, and affects grimace.
(B, ii, 201–202)

The second book is everywhere physical, and Pope constantly finds the most corporeal analogues for what are, after all, nonphysical practices. The lines above are typical in their reduction of mental to physical: flattery of the quill turns into feathery tickling. When a physical analogue is not quite so conveniently visual and tactile, Pope relies on what he might not have hesitated to regard as metaphors of sound.[21] Consequently, in the process of reduction and literalization, bad drama, bad disputation, and bad poetry are all enlisted in the services of the "wond'rous pow'r of Noise" (B, ii, 222). The goddess signals the start of the contest:

> Now thousand tongues are heard in one loud din:
> The Monkey-mimics rush discordant in;
> 'Twas chatt'ring, grinning, mouthing, jabb'ring all,
> And Noise and Norton, Brangling and Breval,
> Dennis and Dissonance, and captious Art,
> And Snip-snap short, and Interruption smart,
> And Demonstration thin, and Theses thick,
> And Major, Minor, and Conclusion quick.
>
> (B, ii, 235–242)

This verbal chaos is a tour de force even for Pope. The manipulation of such terms as "Demonstration thin" and "Theses thick" at the close of the description recalls Touchstone's account of his quarrel at court in *As You Like It*:

I did dislike the cut of a certain courtier's beard. He sent me word, if I said his beard was not cut well, he was in the mind it was: this is called the Retort Courteous. If I sent him word again it was not well cut, he would send me word, he cut it to please himself: this is called the Quip Modest. If again, it was not well cut, he disabled my judgment: this is called the Reply Churlish. . . . If again, it was not well cut, he would say I lied: this is called the Countercheck Quarrelsome: and so to the Lie Circumstantial and the Lie Direct.

(V, iv, 66–77)

Pope uses the inflated terms, as does Shakespeare, for the purpose of comic deflation. But by crowding his terms close upon physical, monosyllabic adjectives and by crowding them into a verse paragraph already laden with "noisy" words, Pope makes them part of an auditory pattern of turgid cacophony which actually represents physically the frenzied confusion it describes. The point is not merely that Pope is capable of using sound to emphasize confusion, for he does that in several places, including the skirmishes of *The Rape of the Lock* and the description of a disordered mob at the opening of Book II:

> A motley mixture! in long wigs, in bags,
> In silks, in crapes, in Garters, and in rags.
>
> (B, ii, 21–22)

< GENERIC CONFUSION >

But he can and does go beyond that technique in the "Noise and Norton" passage to reduce the dunces to dissonance itself.

Finally, all the major elements of literary confusion, indefinite activity, and mire are incorporated in a conceit which Pope added to the revised Book II:

> Thro' Lud's fam'd gates, along the well-known Fleet
> Rolls the black troop, and overshades the street,
> 'Till show'rs of Sermons, Characters, Essays,
> In circling fleeces whiten all the ways:
> So clouds replenish'd from some bog below,
> Mount in dark volumes, and descend in snow.
>
> (B, ii, 359–364)

In the midst of this delicately controlled description the confusion of the dunces and all their works becomes even more apparent by contrast. The miscreants are, as Pope had told his friend they were doomed to be, "swallowd up & drownd in their own Dulness & Dirtiness." The poet is one who fulfills his own prophecies.

4.

At the close of Book II the goddess presides over a reading contest in which the sermons of "Orator" Henley and the epics of Sir Richard Blackmore gradually put everyone to sleep.

> Then down are roll'd the books; stretch'd o'er 'em lies
> Each gentle clerk, and mutt'ring seals his eyes.
> As what a Dutchman plumps into the lakes,
> One circle first, and then a second makes;
> What Dulness dropt among her sons imprest
> Like motion from one circle to the rest;
> So from the mid-most the nutation spreads
> Round and more round, o'er all the sea of heads.
>
> (B, ii, 403–410)

The third book, in which Cibber goes on the duncical equivalent of Aeneas's trip to the underworld, has the world of sleep as both

31

its logical and its imagistic foundation, and it extends several of the implications of the preceding book. In a way it is a psychological culmination of the physical muddle of Book II. Sleep, like mire, reduces all human activity to one dead level of homogeneous disorganization, and for this reason both sleep and mire are regarded by enlightened individuals as conditions to be triumphed over. But for the sons of Dulness, Pope suggests in these two books, slime and slumber *are* the human condition. These states are the natural habitat of duncery, the states in which the dunces (to adapt Wordsworth) are most themselves.

Pope is careful to give the sleep of dunces an especially reductive quality by associating it continually with subhuman intoxication. At the end of the second book the "nutation" of sleep widens to include an indication of how "the nightly Muse" conveyed several "bards" to "stews" and of how Henley not only "seem'd" but was "a Priest in drink." The third book—"nothing but a feverish Dream," according to John Dennis—begins also in drunken sleep:

> But in her Temple's last recess inclos'd,
> On Dulness' lap th' Anointed head repos'd.
> Him close she curtains round with Vapours blue,
> And soft besprinkles with Cimmerian dew.
> Then raptures high the seat of Sense o'erflow,
> Which only heads refin'd from Reason know.
> (B, iii, 1–6)

Lesser reminders of intoxication as a way of life occur throughout the book: Shadwell is twice represented with the "Poppy on his brows" (alluding to the fact that he took opium), Ned Ward is said to be the topic of conversation in "each ale-house . . . each gillhouse . . . And answ'ring gin-shops," and "Hist'ry" is also seen with "her Pot" of ale (B, iii, 22, 317, 147–148, 196).

Within the world of Cibberian sleep itself Pope elaborates upon several of the kinds of confusion that have already appeared. As in Book I, the most striking suggestions of aberration occur in portrayals of monstrous birth. Pope's perverted Garden of Adonis, the "dusky vale" where "poetic souls . . . Demand new bodies,"

< GENERIC CONFUSION >

has been discussed earlier in connection with the first book's Cave of Poverty and Poetry. The theme of both those passages is extended later in Book III in two splendid descriptions of artistic impropriety giving birth (also as in Book I) to natural disorder. In this "prophetic" book Pope's Cibber witnesses the success of various theatrical extravaganzas. At Settle's almost hysterical insistence the laureate first "turn'd aside" his "never-blushing head,"

> And look'd, and saw a sable Sorc'rer rise,
> Swift to whose hand a winged volume flies:
> All sudden, Gorgons hiss, and Dragons glare,
> And ten-horn'd fiends and Giants rush to war.
> Hell rises, Heav'n descends, and dance on Earth:
> Gods, imps, and monsters, music, rage, and mirth,
> A fire, a jigg, a battle, and a ball,
> 'Till one wide conflagration swallows all.
>   (B, iii, 233–240)

These lines are thick with specific satire which glances, for instance, at a flurry of sensational productions including Theobald's *Rape of Proserpine,* and the "sable Sorc'rer" is the Doctor Faustus who had become increasingly popular in what Pope terms "a set of Farces."[22] But Pope at once turns all of this into a myth in miniature by implying that these deformed productions are real, first of all, and that they are actually the productions of Faustus, the result of black magic or "anti-creation." In Book I Pope uses pastoral poetry in which "Realms shift their place" as an emblem of artistic and natural confusion; in this passage the same disorder is at work, but the realms have become cosmic as "Hell rises, Heav'n descends," and both "dance on Earth." The universal and stately dance which John Davies had celebrated in *Orchestra* has degenerated into a frenetic, transitory "jigg."

Following the spectacular scene change of the "wide conflagration" comes one of the descriptive passages of pure loveliness which occur periodically in the *Dunciad* as if to remind the reader that, however tawdry the subject matter, a great poet is still in control of its exposure. The description is in Pope's best pastoral mode:

> Thence a new world to Nature's laws unknown,
> Breaks out refulgent, with a heav'n its own:
> Another Cynthia her new journey runs,
> And other planets circle other suns.
> The forests dance, the rivers upward rise.
> Whales sport in woods, and dolphins in the skies;
> And last, to give the whole creation grace,
> Lo! one vast Egg produces human race.
>
> (B, iii, 241–248)

The matter of the lines, however, is not the pastoral order for which their manner would be appropriate, but instead an order militating against natural distinctions.[23] And again Pope fuses the most particular satire with lines of literally cosmic relevance. The last line, as Pope notes, alludes to a play of Theobald's in which Harlequin had actually emerged—*mirabile visu*—from an egg on stage. But the facts of Pope's note are not intended to prevent us from seeing the larger and more general implications of perverse creation. Indeed, one may even feel that the comment was written to call attention to the poet's myth-making felicity in grandly re-creating this trivial historical event. If that be a poet's pride, it could not be better founded, for the passage is one of the finest in the *Dunciad*.

Pope devotes considerable attention to the contemporary stage, and he was understandably reluctant to relinquish such a fertile analogue. It should be recalled that even in the 1728 *Dunciad*, with its more scholarly hero, Pope had emphasized that Theobald was responsible for theatrical as well as learned dulness. With the coronation of Cibber in 1743 Pope was able to relate theatrical chaos even more directly to his main figure, a man who has prospered as an actor and manager. Consequently there is more immediacy when Settle (in a slightly expanded declaration) tells Cibber later in the third book of great days to come on the boards, for they will involve Cibber personally:

> "Teach thou the warb'ling Polypheme to roar,
> And scream thyself as none e'er scream'd before!
> To aid our cause, if Heav'n thou can'st not bend,

< GENERIC CONFUSION >

Hell thou shalt move; for Faustus is our friend:
Pluto with Cato thou for this shalt join,
And link the Mourning Bride to Proserpine.
Grubstreet! thy fall should men and Gods conspire,
Thy stage shall stand, ensure it but from Fire.
Another Æschylus appears! prepare
For new abortions, all ye pregnant fair!
In flames, like Semele's, be brought to bed,
While op'ning Hell spouts wild-fire at your head."
                                        (B, iii, 305–316)

Faustus again plays his double role as thespian and representative of pandemonium, as both the object of extreme popularity and the emblematic indication that the vox populi is plainly on the side of the wrong angels. The prophesied "abortions" recall the literary abortion and embryo which originally surrounded Cibber in Book I, and, as before, Pope's imagery is designed to suggest that artistic deformity is at once the mirror and source of actual deformity.[24]

Pope is doing more than indicating contemporary theatrical taste is debased. That in itself is sufficient to demonstrate social confusion, and he does wish to point out such confusion and debasement in an age when Cibber "sits Lord Chancellor of Plays" and "Ambrose Philips is prefer'd for Wit" (B, iii, 324, 326). But Pope also wishes to call our attention to the confusion of the individual mind, the confusion of the spirit capable of such activity. When Cibber witnesses the spectacle of Harlequin's stage birth,

Joy fills his soul, joy innocent of thought;
"What pow'r, he cries, what pow'r these wonders wrought?"
                                        (B, iii, 249–250)

Settle's answer reminds us that Pope had called Cibber "monster-breeding" much earlier in the poem and that he did not do so casually:

"Son; what thou seek'st is in thee! Look, and find
Each Monster meets his likeness in thy mind."
                                        (B, iii, 251–252)

This exchange is undeniably comic, but it also represents a profound inversion of the "paradise within thee, happier far" which Milton's Adam is told to seek in *his* mind. Monsters beget monsters, and however oblivious Pope's Cibber may be of his internal condition, his spirit is deformed; however painless his labor may be, the state of his "monster-breeding breast" resembles not Adam's potential harmony, but Satan's "Hell within."[25]

Book III also recalls the more central Genesis of Book I, the procreation in which Dulness herself is directly engaged. At the opening of the poem the goddess is introduced with

> . . . her mighty wings out-spread
> To hatch a new Saturnian age of Lead.

The same image elaborated cuts more deeply into Settle's ecstatic prophecy to Cibber:

> "And see, my son! the hour is on its way,
> That lifts our Goddess to imperial sway;
> This fav'rite Isle, long sever'd from her reign,
> Dove-like, she gathers to her wings again.[26]
> Now look thro' Fate! behold the scene she draws!
> What aids, what armies to assert her cause!
> See all her progeny, illustrious sight!
> Behold, and count them, as they rise to light."
>
> (B, iii, 123–130)

Perhaps what Dulness hatches in this vision "thro' Fate" is the "one vast Egg" which "produces human race." The images complement one another, at any rate, and the boundless fecundity of Dulness is emphasized even more in the third book than in her first appearance. She is characterized as a grotesque counterpart of Cybele, the mythological "Mother of the sky" (131); the new "Mighty Mother" of the *Dunciad*'s first line becomes in Book III the antithetical force to the *magna mater* of the gods: "Behold an hundred sons, and each a Dunce" (138). The scene is set between two worlds—one all but dead, the other more than powerful enough to be born.

< GENERIC CONFUSION >

5.

At several points in Book III we see the sons of Dulness engaged in the same massy physical confusion which dominates Book II, but their activity now begins to assume a more violent and frenzied aspect. This procession of would-be poets, for example, bears little resemblance to the comic contest earlier in the day:

> "Each Songster, Riddler, ev'ry nameless name,
> All crowd, who foremost shall be damn'd to Fame.
> Some strain in rhyme; the Muses, on their racks,
> Scream like the winding of ten thousand jacks:
> Some free from rhyme or reason, rule or check,
> Break Priscian's head, and Pegasus's neck;
> Down, down they larum, with impetuous whirl,
> The Pindars, and the Miltons of a Curl."
>   (B, iii, 157–164)

Part of the reason for the different cast of this description lies in the sheer violence of the imagery: tortures, screams, and fractures, however figurative they may be, will have their sobering effect. It is also true that the last line's intense indignation of incongruity is partly responsible, though Pope had used the latter device in a less troublesome context in Book I when he surveyed "the Classics of an Age that heard of none." But the most ominous element of all is the "impetuous whirl" which directs this entire exercise in destruction. For the most part Pope has previously shown the dunces as bumbling and muddled; their thinking has not become any more ordered, but he begins to indicate here that their very confusion has acquired a unity and an energy of its own. We have seen the dunces before behaving without restraint or decorum; now, in their concerted effort and "impetuous whirl," we see them moving without "rule or check."

Similar images of circular motion occur throughout the third book, and they become an important means of resolving a conceptual paradox—namely, that the dunces exhibit a nonproductive energy (one which does not "go anywhere") and yet are part of an energy which progresses steadily like the "nutation" at the close of Book II. Metaphors of circularity serve, in other words, to characterize physically both the centrifugal energy and centripetal attraction of Dulness.[27] Cibber, in whom the goddess finds "her Image full exprest," naturally partakes of both these qualities. Settle reveals to Cibber his dull apotheosis:

> "As man's Mæanders to the vital spring
> Roll all their tides, then back their circles bring;
> Or whirligigs, twirl'd round by skilful swain,
> Suck the thread in, then yield it out again:
> All nonsense thus, of old or modern date,
> Shall in thee centre, from thee circulate."
>
> (B, iii, 55–60)

As the earthly representative of Dulness, Cibber becomes both the chosen source and end of her power; but John Rich, the "Angel of Dulness," is almost as blessed. Following the stage spectaculars described by Settle, the theatrical manager is portrayed at the center of a similar image of goddess-directed circularity:

> "Immortal Rich! how calm he sits at ease
> 'Mid snows of paper, and fierce hail of pease;
> And proud his Mistress' orders to perform,
> Rides in the whirlwind, and directs the storm."
>
> (B, iii, 261–264)

The image is significant because it is more than derisive; Pope indicates that the whirlwind of bad taste which (to use a word that becomes significant later in the poem) *involves* Rich and the London stage is created according to the dictates of Dulness herself.

Other metaphors of rolling movement encompass the passivity of the dunces and the wrongheaded but coherent activity of Dulness as it involves them. There is, for example, Cibber's metempsychosis:

> "Who knows how long thy transmigrating soul
> Might from Bœotian to Bœotian roll?"
>
> (B, iii, 49–50)

< GENERIC CONFUSION >

or the unchecked progression of the barbarians' destruction of civilization's libraries:

"From shelves to shelves see greedy Vulcan roll,
And lick up all their Physic of the Soul;"
                    (B, iii, 81–82)

or the momentum of Cibberian success:

"Happier thy fortunes! like a rolling stone,
Thy giddy dulness still shall lumber on,
Safe in its heaviness, shall never stray,
But lick up ev'ry blockhead in the way."
                    (B, iii, 293–296)

Most of these images of circular motion are placed in comic contexts or are phrased humorously, and it is only their insistent recurrence which is ominous. But that subliminal insistence, almost as inexorable as the progress of Dulness, is Pope's point. When he at last fulfilled the prophecies of Book III, it was inevitable that the *New Dunciad* would describe how

The gath'ring number, as it moves along,
Involves a vast involuntary throng,
Who gently drawn, and struggling less and less,
Roll in her Vortex, and her pow'r confess.
                    (IV, 81–84)

6.

Book IV of the *Dunciad* has drawn respect and praise from a great many critics of Pope. The "crowded thoughts and stately numbers" which Johnson pointed to at the close of the fourth book are in fact qualities to be found throughout, and the presence of such intellectual range and hieratic or "Miltonic" loftiness has resulted in a continuing interest in both the cultural and poetic backgrounds of the final book. These two concerns are ultimately one: the light of intellectual tradition and the divine illumination which finds its most brilliant expression in

39

Paradise Lost are, for Pope no less than for Milton, emanations of the same order. Discussing the theological and ontological perspective which traditionally connected light with being itself, Mr. Williams concludes:

The promise of Milton's Satan to the monarch of Chaos, then, and the return to Chaos and Darkness which the *Dunciad* celebrates, are more than superficially linked. Milton and Pope are both attempting to dramatize the nature of evil, which in Christian thought aims always at the destruction of creation. Since the universe exists by virtue of the "being" imparted to it by God, and since Chaos and Darkness represent the realm of "non-being," this imaginative restoration is the ultimate destruction—un-creation. No other action could have better realized for Pope's readers the Christian concept of evil—that which is the annihilation and negation of the good. And by no other means could Pope have so readily revealed the evil implicit in duncery as he conceived it than by his parody of *Paradise Lost,* the metaphoric alliance of duncery with diabolism.[28]

Mr. Brower also comments upon Pope's equation of dulness and evil, concluding that Pope's "feeling of the connexion between human folly and larger orders and disorders is religious in a quite primitive sense," and he refers to the fourth book as "an epic fantasia, a series of free variations on the Miltonic theme of 'right reason obscured.' "[29]

The issues of Book IV, then, are clear, frighteningly clear, and fortunately they are still charged with considerable emotion. What is not so clearly grasped, however, is that Book IV is just that—the fourth and final book of a unified poem—and that Pope knew what he was doing in not permitting it to stand alone. Mr. Brower and F. R. Leavis, for example, imply that the *New Dunciad* of 1742 is really too fine for its final resting place, and Mr. Williams is of the opinion that, "with the addition of the fourth book to the original three-book version of the poem, the *Dunciad's* overall structure ultimately breaks down." He sees "some evidence of the discontinuity between the books . . . in the fact that the parody of the 'action' of the Aeneid is not carried over, in any organic fashion, into Book IV."[30]

< GENERIC CONFUSION >

Mr. Williams's assumption about the poem's narrative principles will be discussed later; for the present it is necessary to examine the fundamental imagistic connections between Book IV and the earlier books. This means virtually avoiding the more obvious topic of Pope's "ideas" and allusions in the last book and postponing the more neglected question of structure in the entire poem. But understanding Pope's use of integral imagery in Book IV has much to do with understanding how that book depends upon the rest of the poem and how it becomes more than a Miltonic medley or a pessimistic pastiche.

The first descriptive passage in Book IV suggests initially that Pope has radically altered the poem's physical context. The reader is hurried into a surrealistic wasteland.

> Now flam'd the Dog-star's unpropitious ray,
> Smote ev'ry Brain, and wither'd ev'ry Bay;
> Sick was the Sun, the Owl forsook his bow'r,
> The moon-struck Prophet felt the madding hour:
> Then rose the Seed of Chaos, and of Night,
> To blot out Order, and extinguish Light,
> Of dull and venal a new World to mold,
> And bring Saturnian days of Lead and Gold.
>
> (IV, 9–16)

This is certainly a more sinister landscape than anything encountered previously. The Dog Star, traditionally associated with the season of heat and madness, is here actually endowed with the physical power to cause those states—the power to wither and to smite. This quiet manuever allows Pope two effects not otherwise attainable. He is able to suggest that the Dog Star's "unpropitious ray" is somehow related to the "one dim Ray of Light" he requests in his new invocation. And he is able to create in the description itself the "darkness visible" which he also invokes because he is free to depict night in which there is compelling and even bright ("flam'd") light. Turning Milton's shadowy abstraction, "darkness visible," into an actual poetic visualization is a nice feat in itself, but it has a particular relevance here since

41

it provides an opportunity to observe what is operating beneath the obvious Miltonic allusions.

Despite the atmosphere of intense solemnity those allusions lend to the passage, Pope is actually constructing his physical setting on the same principles he has employed throughout the poem—namely, the principles of contradiction and confusion. Essentially the passage operates in the same fashion as those earlier descriptions where "Realms shift their place" and "Whales sport in woods." And although the bright night and sunless heat of the passage almost automatically evoke intellectual associations (and are meant to), the fact remains that the physical confusion of these elements results in a visual wasteland, and that this wasteland has much in common with the sewage wasteland of Book II which likewise provided both the background and the emblem of confusion.

Continually in the fourth book Pope elaborates upon the types of imagery and the types of imagistic logic which he establishes earlier in the poem. I have noted, for example, that Pope uses a rapid series of animated personifications in Book I to illustrate fundamental violations of kind:

> She sees a Mob of Metaphors advance,
> Pleas'd with the madness of the mazy dance:
> How Tragedy and Comedy embrace:
> How Farce and Epic get a jumbled race.

In Book IV a similarly crowded scene evolves into a vast iconographic survey of the varieties of human endeavor:

> Beneath her foot-stool, *Science* groans in Chains,
> And *Wit* dreads Exile, Penalties and Pains.
> There foam'd rebellious *Logic,* gagg'd and bound,
> There, stript, fair *Rhet'ric* languish'd on the ground;
> His blunted Arms by *Sophistry* are born,
> And shameless *Billingsgate* her Robes adorn.
> *Morality*, by her false Guardians drawn,
> *Chicane* in Furs, and *Casuistry* in Lawn,
> Gasps, as they straiten at each end of the cord,
> And dies, when Dulness gives her page the word.

< GENERIC CONFUSION >

Mad *Mathesis* alone was unconfin'd,
Too mad for mere material chains to bind,
Now to pure Space lifts her extatic stare,
Now running round the Circle, finds it square.
But held in ten-fold bonds the *Muses* lie,
Watch'd both by Envy's and by Flatt'ry's eye:
There to her heart sad Tragedy addrest
·The dagger wont to pierce the Tyrant's breast;
But sober History restrain'd her rage,
And promis'd Vengeance on a barb'rous age.
There sunk Thalia, nerveless, cold, and dead,
Had not her Sister Satyr held her head.

(IV, 21–42)

The comic vivacity of the first book's "mazy dance" is largely absent here because Knowledge ("Science") and her main attributes have been enchained as traitors to the new government. But Pope is careful to keep the scene alive. Not only does he include the sketch of "Mad Mathesis"—to whom the adjective "extatic" bears its radical meaning—"running round the Circle," but he also creates as much of an actively "jumbled race" as his narrative will allow by sowing his lines thickly with "figures ill pair'd" like those of Book I. Despite the static elements essential to the scene, Pope crowds his stage to suggest the same kinetic confusion we are accustomed to. The mere lineal fact that "*Sophistry*" follows close upon "*Rhet'ric,*" or that "*Morality*" is so closely compassed round by "*Chicane*" and "*Casuistry*" is enough to render their indiscriminate mingling palpable.

But the "Chains" are a very graphic part of this visualization, and Pope is equally attentive to vivifying the details of violent and unnatural repression. The various fetters become more than a casual metaphor when we find that "Science *groans* in Chains," that Logic "*foam'd*" having been "*gagg'd* and *bound*," that Morality "*gasps*," and that the Muses "*lie*" (Pope's infrequent puns usually have a telling inevitability) in their "ten-fold bonds." And the chains become even more somber if we recall that they represent here a profound inversion of the usual role of fetters in the iconography Pope was heir to. One conventional seven-

teenth-century engraving, for example, which serves as the frontis-
piece to the translation by Monmouth of Senault's *The Use of
the Passions*, and which Pope probably saw,[31] depicts Reason
seated on the throne that Dulness has assumed in Pope's portrait. Beneath *Reason*'s "foot-stool" slack but sturdy chains lead
down to personifications of the various passions who constitute
a harmonious miniature kingdom. This particular engraving is
merely a rather literal extension of a Renaissance tradition in
which, according to Erwin Panofsky, slaves and apes in chains
commonly represented the subjection of "everything subhuman
in man."[32]

Pope undoubtedly uses his grand metaphor of unnatural bondage, then, with an acute awareness of the associations it will bear.
It represents the ultimate reversal of a familiar visual as well as
philosophical concept, and he employs minor variations on the
same imagistic theme throughout Book IV as images of similarly
wrongheaded repression are invariably associated with militant
violations of vital generic distinctions.

Thus even effete Opera, personified as a tawdry "Harlot form
. . . With mincing step . . . too pretty much to stand," has sufficient repressive strength to claim that the new Phoebus "dances in
my chains" (IV, 45–62). The blindly standardized education en-
forced by Dr. Busby likewise has the power to "hand one jingling
padlock on the mind" (IV, 162). This sort of rigidity is not only
oppressive, of course, but "uncreating" as well, and its destructive aspect becomes even more apparent in Bentley's proud display of pedagogical perversity. The concept of rigid bondage
takes on a new visual manifestation:

> "We only furnish what he cannot use,
> Or wed to what he must divorce, a Muse:
> Full in the midst of Euclid dip at once,
> And *petrify* a Genius to a Dunce:
> Or set on Metaphysic ground to prance,
> Show all his paces, not a step advance.
> With the same *Cement*, ever sure to *bind*,
> We bring to one dead level ev'ry mind."
>   (IV, 261–268; my italics)

< GENERIC CONFUSION >

And once this stultifying petrifaction has been brought to its conclusion,

> "Then take him to devellop, if you can,
> And hew the Block off, and get out the Man."
>
> (IV, 269–270)

The last line alludes to the Neoplatonic idea that each block of marble contained the form of a man, which it was the sculptor's task to liberate. But Bentley and his colleagues reverse the process of liberation and, therefore, of creation.

A more profound philosophical uncreation results later in the book from the mental rigidity of doctrinaire argument; the avowedly agnostic clerk, "prompt to impose, and fond to dogmatize," celebrates the glories of the new logic:

> "We nobly take the high Priori Road,
> And reason downward, till we doubt of God:
> Make Nature still incroach upon his plan;
> And shove him off as far as e'er we can:
> Thrust some Mechanic Cause into his place;
> Or bind in Matter, or diffuse in Space.
> Or, at one bound o'er-leaping all his laws,
> Make God Man's Image, Man the final Cause."
>
> (IV, 471–478)

The clerk's error is obviously one of pride, and the passage recalls famous parallels from the *Essay on Man*. But even more relevant is Pope's success with physical verbs that render the violence and inflexibility of such self-imposition. The devotees of mental rigidity force their own way: they *take, make, shove,* and *thrust* where they should proceed reverentially, and they *bind, o'er-leap,* and re-*make* their Maker. They act, in short, without the least discrimination. Samuel Johnson, describing what he believed to be an indiscriminate aesthetic, would later say that "the most heterogeneous ideas are yoked by violence together"; Pope characterizes an indiscriminate philosophy through metaphors of indiscriminate binding, through more tangible forms of Johnson's intellectualized image. The result, finally, of all this misplaced binding is inevitably misshapen humanity:

> "First *slave* to Words, then *vassal* to a Name,
> Then dupe to Party; child and man the same;
> *Bounded* by Nature, *narrow'd* still by Art,
> A trifling head, and a *contracted* heart."
> (IV, 501–504; my italics)

However different in emotive force the images of rigidity in Book IV may be from earlier descriptions of confusion, they are not fundamental departures. With the fulfillment of the third book's prophecy it is as if the whole poem "sets": the embryo and abortion of Book I now settle into contracted maturity; the mud in Book II hardens to "Cement"; the "Nonsense precipitate, like running lead" in the first book solidifies eventually into "ten-fold bonds." The images are not essentially new; they are familiar ones allowed to run to their logical completion.

I suggested earlier how one of the most memorable metaphors of Book IV, the "Vortex" of Dulness which "involves a vast involuntary throng," grows naturally out of similar metaphors in Book III of circular energy—both whirling and rolling. All of these images imply not only confusion but confusion with a purpose, motion with a goal or center. They suggest, in other words, that Dulness ultimately exerts a kind of magnetic attraction over the entire landscape of the poem, and this implication becomes clearer when one recalls that the pattern of imagery extends back even further to Cibber's original prayer in Book I:

> "O thou! of Bus'ness the directing soul!
> To this our head like byass to the bowl,
> Which, as more pond'rous, make its aim more true,
> Obliquely wadling to the mark in view."
> (B, i, 169–172)

What happens, basically, in Book IV is that the "mark in view" becomes even more visible and attractive for even more votaries, and their "aim" becomes even "more true":

> The young, the old, who feel her inward sway,
> One instinct seizes, and transports away.
> None need a guide, by sure Attraction led,
> And strong impulsive gravity of Head:

< GENERIC CONFUSION >

None want a place, for all their Centre found,
Hung to the Goddess, and coher'd around.
Not closer, orb in orb, conglob'd are seen
The buzzing Bees about their dusky Queen.

(IV, 73–80)

The closing couplet, in addition to converting the dunces into passive and sexless drones, recalls a similar metaphoric expression of mindless, confused crowding in Book III where huddled the "millions and millions" of "poetic souls" awaiting birth, "As thick as bees o'er vernal blossoms fly" (B, iii, 33). The passage as a whole looks back to the more general metaphor, elaborated from Book I onward, of confused but powerful progress. The oblique "wadling" has been accelerated by "sure Attraction" and "impulsive gravity"; but the later passage develops inevitably out of the movement of Book I, where the "byass" has been present from the beginning.

In addition to connecting the fourth book metaphorically with the preceding books, the lines quoted above also provide the logical basis for the last book itself. It is because Pope finally develops to its full extent the concept of "sure Attraction"—nascent in the earlier books—that the *Dunciad*'s famous closing paragraph can operate with such intellectual complexity and emotional intensity. The telling phrases which carry that paragraph to Universal Darkness, phrases such as "resistless falls," or "at her felt approach," or "secret might," are successful because Pope has already charged them with a plausible and "impulsive gravity" of their own. But the "sure Attraction—Vortex" passage (IV, 73–84) has an even more comprehensive function in the last book because it at once sets the stage and fully predetermines the mode of activity that is to follow. Since the stage has been designated as the point where "all their Centre found," where all are "coher'd" and "conglob'd," the passage provides the perfect prologue for the long parade of crowded confusion which is the subject of Book IV. And since *all* are "by sure Attraction led," it is perfectly logical that the long pageant which unfolds should be one where there is a parade in which

> . . . march'd the bard and blockhead, side by side,
> Who rhym'd for hire, and patroniz'd for pride;
>
> (IV, 101–102)

a procession in which we might see,

> . . . thick as Locusts black'ning all the ground,
> A tribe, with weeds and shells fantastic crown'd;
>
> (IV, 397–398)

or where we might watch

> The learned Baron Butterflies design,
> Or draw to silk Arachne's subtile line;
> The Judge to dance his brother Sergeant call;
> The Senator at Cricket urge the Ball.
>
> (IV, 589–592)

And it is also logical, as it has been throughout the *Dunciad*, that the crowding of such "figures ill pair'd" should be indicative of a larger generic confusion, of insistent violations of natural distinctions. Near the end of the *Dunciad* a high "Priest" of Dulness performs several "specious miracles" through which he "turns Hares to Larks, and Pigeons into Toads" (IV, 554). By the end of the poem it has become clear that all of the works of the dunces are "specious miracles" which dissolve nature's genres. Their apotheosis can only come as it does, with the arrival of the "all-composing Hour" in which all differences are settled and the "great Anarch" restores her "dread Empire."

7.

At least one influential critic of Augustan satire has complained of disunity in the subject matter of the *Dunciad*. Mr. Jack claims that, "while the last Book has a wide scope and a serious moral purpose, the first three Books are primarily concerned with Dulness in literature and are largely retaliatory in intention."[33] This statement demonstrates a fundamental misunderstanding of several issues. Most obviously mistaken is the

< GENERIC CONFUSION >

assumption that satire which deals largely in terms of literature and personalities is consequently—"Major, Minor, and Conclusion quick"—incapable of possessing "wide scope" or "serious moral purpose."

It is certainly true that the first three books are more "literary" than Book IV in the sense that they are crowded with the names of authors and booksellers. But Pope, as we have seen, constantly places literary aberrations and their perpetrators in a larger metaphorical context of unnatural creation—that is, uncreation. However specific the satire may be at points, Pope never loses sight of the broader poetic conception. In fact, Pope's most "specific" passages are usually the points at which his poetry becomes broadest in its imagistic evocation. (Maynard Mack has most recently commented on "that special dignity which seems always to characterize his verse when passion coalesces ideally with poetic role.")[34] So, for example, the description of what seems to be a particular play by a particular playwright is simultaneously a description of a "new world, to Nature's laws unknown." When we see over and over in the poem that literary confusion becomes emblematic, on the strength of Pope's consistent metaphorical system, of an all-embracing confusion, it makes little sense to speak of the "exclusively literary bearing" of any of the books of the *Dunciad*.[35]

I labor this argument only because Mr. Jack's misreading of the *Dunciad* illustrates how essential it is to first understand the poetry if one is to understand the satire. T. S. Eliot did not invent the "objective correlative." It has always been a requisite of good poetry, and for Pope, an unusually literary poet, the literature of his day provided what now seems an inevitable correlative for a poem about civilization and un-civilization. In Book IV of the *Dunciad* Pope's vision of anti-literature becomes more clearly a vision of the anti-Word as well. It is difficult to imagine a more "unified" progression.

In a more general context, Mr. Brower remarks that "for Pope at the start of his career, as at the end, the imitation of life is also the imitation of literature."[36] We might consider too, in the context of the *Dunciad*, that for Pope the confusion of literature is also the confusion of life. This intimate conceptual connection is maintained consistently throughout the poem. The most fundamental mode of implying this relation is the system of physical imagery which brings literary endeavor and all other human endeavor to the same level. But Pope also represents the connection more explicitly by merely combining his topics: there is, for example, theological discussion in the earlier books, just as there is "literary" discussion in Book IV. It is necessary to remember that as early as Book II Pope had compared Cibber (and Theobald before him) to another "Antichrist of wit" (B, ii, 16). Conversely, it is significant that the activity of Book IV begins (45ff) with the entrance of Italian Opera, who is depicted as a prostitute "in patch-work flutt'ring" because her very presence in England, her successful patchwork eclecticism, violates the decorum of generic kinds. Flaunting her misconceived manifesto —"One trill shall harmonize joy, grief, and rage"—she serves as the reiterative emblem of an aesthetic and a society in which "Tragedy and Comedy embrace" and "Farce and Epic get a jumbled race."

< CHAPTER TWO >

"The Miltons
of a Curl"
Epic Inversion

Pope's use of bad literature and bad writers as both symptom and symbol of a more pervasive cultural confusion rests upon a rather modern attitude. Our own assumption that literature, whatever else it may do, inevitably reflects important truths concerning the society which produced it is a critical premise that did not attain firm footing until the Restoration. Of course literature had long been regarded as a source of historical information, and inquiring readers might find, for example, contemporary allusion in Virgil's poetry, an interesting if fragmentary record of the facts of life under Augustus. But toward the end of the seventeenth century incidental antiquarianism began to develop into a fuller sense of the past. The more general "spirit" of a literary work (as well as its factual allusions) became a matter of historical import and interest. It was shortly after the Restoration that the important phrase "the genius of the age" came into being, and the step to the idea of "the spirit of the age" was neither drastic nor distant.[1]

The historical self-consciousness and growing critical sophistication that followed the Renaissance were molded by Dryden and lesser men into a unified, contextual approach to aesthetic productivity. Criticism which before had been primarily rhetorical began to yield to what we now call literary history, and literary history necessarily became inseparable from history as a whole. Faced with a recent and all too obvious cleavage in their own history and literature, the major critics of the Restoration period sought to "place" their own age in the continuum of Western civilization, and one result of this endeavor was the gradual emergence of our own historical perspective and relativism—the point of view, for example, in which literature comes to be considered at least partly as the expression of a particular society.

Pope's commentary to his translation of Homer is a continuing discussion of this sort. He sees the *Iliad* and *Odyssey* as the grand record of a civilization "almost three thousand Years" distant; in fact, he calls Homer's poems "the only true mirror of that ancient World." Pope's claim is in part informed by the traditional notion that the poetry of Homer was a compendium of Greek knowledge, but there is also a recognition that these most "universal" of poems contain fascinatingly "dated" elements peculiar to the time and place of their inception. And when Pope a few years later confronts Shakespeare, that other "universal" genius, his estimate is charged with a certain cultural relativism: "To judge . . . of Shakespeare by Aristotle's rules is like trying a man by the laws of one country who acted under those of another."[2] Pope is attempting to excuse Shakespeare from censure, but he is also attempting, as Dryden had, to indicate that Elizabethan literature is fundamentally different from the literature of ancient Greece, that they "mirror" very different cultures.

Pope was no critical pioneer, and the importance of his perspective is that it is more or less representative of Augustan assumptions about literature. So, for example, when Addison looks back scornfully at an age notorious for its "monkish" forms of literature he is making a social criticism as well as a literary observation.[3] And when Pope looks out at an age which he sees producing reams of literary "abortion" he is making a less comfortable judgment about his own culture, a judgment based on the same evaluative premise that an age which produces corrupt literature is fundamentally corrupt. In itself this connection is an

< EPIC INVERSION >

intellectual abstraction, and thus we see Pope in the *Dunciad* using the full resources and resonances of his art to render it a poetic reality. Wherever possible Pope links literary miscreation with more elemental forms of confusion, from the poem's vision of artistic abortions and "sooterkins" to the eventual uncreation of nature itself.

1.

This connection is conveyed most vividly by the *Dunciad*'s consistent imagistic structure. But the poem's narrative structure is an important part of the meaning too, and Pope did not intend that his "fable" should go unnoticed. The entire narrative of the *Dunciad* stands as an implicit, highly sophisticated criticism of contemporary literature and contemporary society. In various sections of the *Dunciad* Pope points to emblematic perversions in specific kinds of literature, such as party writing, unnatural pastoral, extravagant drama, and opera. Pope turns all of these into analogous physical absurdities—the "dark dexterity of groping well," for example, or the "one wide Conflagration" which "swallows all"—and thus transforms thematic material into vividly metaphorical material. But the chief literary genre in the Augustan hierarchy, and therefore the kind of writing which would be felt to best mirror a culture, was the epic. The *Dunciad* as a narrative whole comments on this form, on the epic in Augustan society.

Within the *Dunciad* contemporary drama provides an especially apt literary and cultural analogue, and Cibber himself provides an apt protagonist as a well-known theatrical manager, author, and arbiter. Yet one of the most conspicuous of the lesser figures in the *Dunciad* is Sir Richard Blackmore, an author who had no connection with the theater and little connection with scandal. Sir Richard was, however, the most prolific of would-be epic poets in the Augustan period: his "indefatigable Muse," Pope notes, "produced no less than six Epic poems."[4] Ever since his ill-advised "Satyr against Wit" (1700) Blackmore had been a standard object of the wits' satires, and he had offended both Pope and Swift; his appearance in the *Dunciad*, therefore, was inevitable.[5] But personal animus must have played a relatively small part in Pope's choice, for he had many more vehement enemies than Blackmore in the years immediately preceding 1728; moreover, when much later the *Dunciad* took its final form, in which Pope eliminated or lessened the roles of other deceased dunces, the physician-poet had been dead for nearly fourteen years. Sir Richard, evidently, had assumed a kind of symbolic importance in Pope's conception of dulness. As a hack writer who gratuitously dared to court not only Calliope but also Urania, Blackmore was for Pope the epitome of "the Miltons of a Curl" who unwittingly damned the society which encouraged their writing and publishing.

Consequently Blackmore's is one of the first names to appear in the *Dunciad*. As Dulness complacently reviews the "sure succession" of duncery, insistent early in Book I, she notices

> . . . old Pryn in restless Daniel shine,
> And Eusden eke out Blackmore's endless line.
> (B, i, 103–104)

Sir Richard's "endless line," at once poetic and cultural, is in both respects a persistent part of the Great Tradition of Dulness. In Book II he appears again as the "everlasting Blackmore" (302) who excels in sheer quantity and volume:

> But far o'er all, sonorous Blackmore's strain;
> Walls, steeples, skies, bray back to him again.
> In Tot'nam fields, the brethren, with amaze,
> Prick all their ears up, and forget to graze;
> Long Chanc'ry-lane retentive rolls the sound,
> And courts to courts return it round and round;
> Thames wafts it thence to Rufus' roaring hall,
> And Hungerford re-echoes bawl for bawl.
> All hail him victor in both gifts of song,
> Who sings so loudly, and who sings so long.
> (B, ii, 259–268)

< EPIC INVERSION >

The ludicrous repetition in the last line and in the line "And courts to courts return it round and round" serves almost as a kind of refined indirect discourse to suggest the pretentious emptiness of "sonorous Blackmore's strain." Blackmore is like the phantom poet whom the booksellers greedily pursue earlier in the same book, poets whose "sounding strain" is "senseless, lifeless! idol void and vain!" Pope would again express the idea of Blackmore's conspicuous emptiness onomatopoetically in the first of his Horatian imitations. Advised by the Friend to write heroic poetry in "CAESAR's Praise," Pope asks indignantly,

> What? like Sir *Richard,* rumbling, rough and fierce,
> With ARMS, and GEORGE, and BRUNSWICK crowd the Verse?
> Rend with tremendous Sound your ears asunder,
> With Gun, Drum, Trumpet, Blunderbuss & Thunder?
>
> (Satire II, i, 23–26)

At the close of the second book of the *Dunciad* this same sonorous vapidity brings the "high heroic Games" to a drowsy halt. Blackmore turns the epic—long considered an ideal means of exciting virtue and valor—into an effective soporific. His "potent Arthur" (either his *Prince Arthur* or *King Arthur,* or both) is the origin of that "nutation" which "spreads Round and more round" until finally, "the soft gifts of Sleep conclude the day." Thus when Pope claims that he has taken Sir Richard Blackmore as his "authority" in "Heroic poetry,"[6] we should be prepared for irony of the most comprehensive sort.

2.

These specific allusions to Blackmore do not, I think, represent the full extent of his role in the *Dunciad.* Although there is no way of "proving" it, I will attempt to show that the broader "action" of the *Dunciad* is an extended criticism of Blackmore and the poetically impoverished practitioners who, like him, have lost sight of any form of heroic action. I have remarked earlier that there is no action, but only activity, in the narrative of the

Dunciad. Its protagonist is entirely passive: he soliloquizes, sees visions, and sleeps. From the "mazy dance" of Book I to the "Vortex" of Book IV the poem contains a vast amount of fragmentary energy and passive inertia, but no unified action. And this very fact has been, as I have noted, the basis for considerable criticism of the *Dunciad*. Speaking of the adverse appraisals of Dennis and Warton, Mr. Sutherland remarks, "It might be replied that Pope is parodying epic action by having almost no action at all; but such a reply would scarcely meet the objection felt."[7] But we can see, I believe, that Pope is parodying not "epic action" itself but rather various *contemporary* ideas concerning epic and heroic endeavor. This becomes clearer when we consider that the generally heterodox opinions of Sir Richard Blackmore regarding the epic constitute a mass of criticism which Pope could only view as fatally misguided.

Blackmore's pronouncements on epic are in large part a repetition of accepted clichés, but, as in his poetry, Sir Richard had a talent for being wrong where it mattered most. For example, however vague the terms might become, nearly all critics of Pope's day regarded the "fable" or "action" as the very foundation or "soul" of an epic poem.[8] But in his own redefinition of the genre Blackmore casually rejects this conventional view of heroic narration: "An Epick Poem is a probable, marvellous, and devis'd Story of an important Enterprize, or great Suffering of some illustrious Person, recited in Verse of the sublime Stile, to afford Delight and Instruction." He further explains, "I have left out the Term *Action*, and have added *Enterprize* or *Suffering*," and then refers us to his earlier claim that action is not an essential part of epic: "It is evident, that none of these Criticks have enquir'd into the Grounds and Foundation of this Maxim, That the Hero must be always a fighting, or at least, an active Person: They have, from one Generation to another, taken this Assertion upon content, and rely'd upon a continu'd Chain and uninterrupted Succession of Authority down from *Aristotle*'s Days to the present Age." Finally Blackmore concludes that the protagonist of an epic need only be an "eminent Sufferer."[9]

< EPIC INVERSION >

This notion of passivity being laudable strikes of course at the heart of traditional epic, and it is not surprising that John Dennis was quick to challenge Blackmore on this point. A few months after the publication of Blackmore's "Essay on the Nature and Constitution of Epick Poetry," Dennis replied with his characteristic blend of colloquialism and learning: "For my part, I have no Notion, that a Suffering Hero can be proper for Epick Poetry. *Milton* could make but very little, even of a Suffering God, who makes quite another Impression with his Lightning and his Thunder in *Paradise Lost*, than with his Meekness and his Stoicism in *Paradise Regain'd*: That great Spirit which Heroick Poetry requires, flows from great Passions and from great Actions." Dennis suggests, significantly, that Blackmore's too inclusive conception of greatness is precisely the wrong thing for the lethargic condition of contemporary society: "But for your part, Sir, that you may deserve more and more of your Country and of Mankind, make Choice of a Hero, whose every Action may flow from those noble Principles and Reform a degenerate Age, which seems so fond of Slavery."[10] It seems that in the *Dunciad* Pope intentionally employs Blackmore's mistaken precept concerning epic and inaction in order to depict Dennis's "degenerate Age . . . so fond of Slavery." In other words, he ironically uses duncical critical theory and representative, contemporaneous subject matter to show that such a combination will result in exactly the opposite of genuine epic. In the *Dunciad* the pert but passive darling of a degenerate age (attended by his like-minded followers) "suffers" complacently and performs nothing.

Other tenets of Blackmorean heterodoxy are also put to ironic use in the *Dunciad*. Although virtually every epic theorist had recognized that Achilles and even Aeneas were not incarnations of flawless virtue, Blackmore took an extreme and generally unacceptable position by claiming that the "hero" of an epic need not be either good or heroic. In 1695 Blackmore had announced that "there is no Necessity the *Hero* should be a good or a wise Person," and that *"Courage"* alone "is sufficient to make the Hero." By 1716 he arrived at a more idiosyncratic position and was uncomfortable even with the word "hero": "The generality of Persons think, that the Conception of a Hero denotes, besides the Idea of Courage, some extraordinary Vertues; and 'tis hard to free the Mind from this Complication when that Term is offer'd to it; and therefore I wish that in speaking of Epick Subjects, Men would lay aside the Word Hero, because of its ambiguous Signification, and use in its place, either Chief Person, Actor, or Warrior, which would not tempt the Reader to expect a Man of uncommon Merit."[11] In each of the important qualifications, Pope's Cibber (and Theobald before him) is dishonorably close to Blackmore's "ideal" epic figure: he is inactive, amoral, unintelligent, and eminently unheroic. Yet Blackmore had insisted upon the protagonist's conspicuous "courage"—to the exclusion of other qualities—and Cibber does possess its urban, middle-class equivalent: his "never-blushing head" continually reminds the reader of his self-assured and shameless "pertness."

Nevertheless Cibber performs so little in the *Dunciad* that even his role as "Chief Person"—in Sir Richard's terms—is problematic. Is he in fact the poem's protagonist? Pope is certainly aware of the ambiguity, and he consistently draws our attention to Cibber's inaction. We are reminded in the prose "Argument," for example, that Cibber does not even initiate the games of Book II. But more relevant is Pope's reworking of the poem's opening lines. The "Tibbald" version begins with a rather close imitation of the opening lines of the *Aeneid*:

> Books and the Man I sing, the first who brings
> The Smithfield Muses to the Ear of Kings.

In Pope's final conception, however, the human protagonist diminishes considerably further:

> The Mighty Mother, and her Son who brings
> The Smithfield Muses to the ear of Kings,
> I sing.

Although many of Warburton's notes to the 1743 *Dunciad* are notoriously heavy-handed, pompous, misleading, or all three, his annotation of the latter invocation is worth consideration: "The

< EPIC INVERSION >

Reader ought here to be cautioned, that the *Mother*, and not the *Son*, is the principal Agent of this Poem: The latter of them is only chosen as her Collegue (as was anciently the custom in Rome before some great Expedition) the main action of the Poem being by no means the Coronation of the Laureate, which is performed in the very first book, but the Restoration of the Empire of Dulness in Britain, which is not accomplished 'till the last."[12]

The preeminence of Dulness herself in the *Dunciad*'s narrative structure brings us to yet another of Blackmore's untraditional contentions—namely, that the protagonist of an epic could be a woman. Elaborating upon his definition of epic, Blackmore remarks: "I have said *Illustrious Person*, to leave the Definition free, and not restrain'd to a Hero; since no Reason, as I believe, can be assign'd, why a Heroine may not be the Principal Person of an Epick, as well as a Tragick Poem, to which it is so nearly ally'd. It is evident, That the essential Properties of an Heroick Work may be all preserv'd, and the principal End of the Poet be as effectually obtain'd, where an illustrious Woman is introduc'd as the chief Character, as well as where a Prince or General sustain that Province."[13] Blackmore's heterodoxy is again significant because it represents more than a critical quibble: it suggests a basic ideological rift. For the Augustan humanist the greatness of the epic and the epic hero lay in the fact that the "one, great, and remarkable action" performed in such works might be regarded as a broadly political accomplishment affecting an entire society (or, in the rather troublesome case of *Paradise Lost*, as an action concerning all of mankind). In this scheme of things, active males won the decisive battles (for better or worse) and founded countries. The women who are important in the major epics are important because they represent passive and potentially destructive forces which could upset the political enterprise at hand. Helen and Circe and Dido all embody a parochial, domestic selfishness which threatens the execution of a larger and more "significant" achievement.

This is admittedly an oversimplification of the epic as well as the Augustan attitudes toward it; but it is clear that Blackmore's conception of the epic did not include the usual estimation of significant social accomplishment performed by an essentially virtuous, active man. In place of this coherent idea he substituted "epic" criteria which condoned inactivity, amorality, and femininity on the part of the epic's "Chief Person." And Pope provides precisely these characteristics in his own anti-epic. Blackmore's criteria accurately define the *Dunciad* whether we regard Cibber or Dulness as the protagonist; for Cibber and Dulness, Pope found, were the same. In the context of the *Dunciad* there is an almost biological truth enclosed in the couplet which links the laureate and the "Mighty Mother":

> In each she marks her Image full exprest,
> But chief in BAYS's monster-breeding breast.
>
> (B, i, 107–108)

We see Cibber as the most eminent of the sublunary progenitors of dull things, as the earthly version of the "Mighty Mother" herself.

The final point of correspondence between Blackmore's epic theory and Pope's anti-epic practice involves the nature of the epic conclusion. Sir Richard was virtually alone also in his opinion that an epic need not conclude happily or successfully: "There is no Necessity that the Hero should finish the Action with Victory and Renown, if we reflect, that the end of the Epick Poet may be equally attain'd, tho the Event should be unfortunate." In fact, says Blackmore, an unhappy ending may even be preferable since "various and important Instructions will arise as well from a calamitous as a happy Issue, and which perhaps will have a better Effect and leave a more lasting Impression on the Mind."[14] One certain method of demonstrating the absurdity of a dubious proposition is to stretch it to its logical extreme. Pope's final triumph of "universal Darkness" is the ironically logical extreme of the sort of "calamitous" epic conclusion which might stir the passions of a Blackmore.

It is significant, then, that Pope's most obvious violations of epic decorum—the essential passivity and inglorious amorality of

< EPIC INVERSION >

Cibber, the femininity of the *Dunciad*'s "Mighty Mother," and the catastrophe of the poem's conclusion—were all recommended quite seriously by the most earnest representative of Augustan epic. But the remarkable correspondence between Pope's poetic plotting and Blackmore's critical plodding does not ultimately "explain" or "account for" the narrative structure of the *Dunciad*. As usual, the specific target at which Pope directed his irony was one that could be endowed with more than local meaning. To assume he was willing to exert his most sustained energies for the sole purpose of satirizing Blackmore would be to assume he was obsessed with discrediting a poet and critic who did not need discrediting in 1728 and who by 1743 was rapidly becoming the literary curiosity he is today. Pope was not one to waste his efforts. But a consideration of what Blackmore represented for Pope may tell us something about the genesis and intention of the *Dunciad*.

Perhaps Sir Richard's most valuable contribution to English literature is that he helped to define Pope's maturing fascination with the obverse side of poetic capability. The poet of the *Dunciad* is primarily interested not in what he considers to be mediocrity—this is not the poem in which to anatomize an Addison—but rather in what he can regard and depict as precisely the opposite of good writing and good thinking. Pope's best prose satire, the *Peri Bathous* (1727) is often described as the "prelude" to the *Dunciad*, and this description is particularly apt if we consider the relevance of the *Peri Bathous* not only to the stages and strategy of the "war of the dunces" but also to Pope's intellectual development.[15] In that mock treatise we see him for the first time exploring the full reaches of antithetical logic. If there is a coherent theory which accounts for sublime poetry, then must not there be a comprehensive theory of the bathetic, a "logical" anti-aesthetic? Pope's reply, of course, is an elaborate affirmation written in fine "treatise" style and in which citations from contemporary poets exemplify the "art of sinking in poetry." And when Pope declares his intention of leading the reader "step by step" down to "the *Bathos*"—which he calls "the Bottom, the End, the

Central Point, the *non plus ultra,* of true Modern Poesie"—he is pointing the way to a logically upside-down world.[16]

Flashes of personal retaliation and provocation are to be seen throughout the *Peri Bathous,* but the unchallenged champion of the treatise's inverted hierarchy is Blackmore. Passages from his poems provide some forty-three different instances of the art of bathos, thus leaving Ambrose Philips, quoted only nineteen times, a distant second. More importantly, Chapter XV (Pope's ironic "Receipt to make an Epic Poem") specifically satirizes Blackmore as the source of wrongheaded epic theory and practice.[17] This short essay, appearing in the *Guardian* in 1713, indicates Pope's early interest in both Blackmore and the mode of ironic inversion, which he uses there to criticize Blackmore and other "mechanick" moderns. Blackmore played an early and important part in shaping Pope's vision of duncery.

In the *Dunciad* Pope's conception grows into a profound inversion of epic structure and heroic content. Thus the amoral and mindless Cibber moves and sleeps in a degenerate world of inaction. Pope's narrative is essentially the story of somnambulent dulness ending in a disintegrating nightmare of uncreation. There is only a termination, not a conclusion, because there is no conventional "action" to be concluded. The "restoration" of the empire of Dulness, or the process of uncivilization, is the poem's larger subject. Action is the change from one state of existence to another, but the movement described in the *Dunciad* is from being to nothingness. This story Pope tells by using a device directly antithetical to the usual "fable" of epic, for the condition at the end of the *Dunciad* is brought about by inaction rather than action. This is not, of course, to say that no one does anything in the poem; but the dunces do no more than what comes naturally. Unlike the heroes of true epic, the dunces are products rather than masters of their environment. Pope knows, as Virgil knew before him, that civilization has to be made, while its unmaking requires only the unresisted contagion of drowsiness. In place of the epic's conscious, heroic action there is only unconscious, inglorious passivity in the *Dunciad*; in place

< EPIC INVERSION >

of the epic's human action signifying a cultural accomplishment there is only subhuman acquiescence signifying Nothing.

Clearly the *Dunciad* does not "use" epic in the same way as the *Rape of the Lock*. In the earlier poem the epic background points up the miniature proportion of Belinda's "rape," and, miniature or not, the action is real and recognizable. But in the *Dunciad* Pope employs epic echoes and parallels in order to portray an inverted world rather than a miniature social sphere. Unlike the "fable" of the *Rape of the Lock*, the plot of the *Dunciad* does not include its actors in an "exquisitely diminished" action.[18] Instead the narrative indicates that the characters are literally the *counter-parts* of active heroes, that they are capable only of destructive passivity, of undoing, of negative action. This explains why Pope does not attempt to construct an entire miniature epic and why he chooses only to imitate various parts of the great epics: the standard invocation, the heroic games, a few well-known speeches, and the prophetic books of the *Aeneid* and *Paradise Lost*. He intentionally imitates those elements of the epics which are static and which are not properly parts of the "action" itself in order to emphasize the "Vis inertiae"[19] of duncery.

Such was not Pope's intention in the *Rape of the Lock*, for the subject and actors were much slighter. Maynard Mack, observing that both poems unmask superficiality, eloquently distinguishes their modes: "In the *Rape of the Lock* it is done with tenderness, a sense of the endearing charm of mortal foibles, for one does not impale a butterfly upon an ax; but in the *Dunciad* it is done with indignation, for one does not survey the dry rot in a whole society through the rainbow wings of sylphs."[20] The metaphorical atmosphere of the *Dunciad* is a world apart from that of the *Rape of the Lock*. This difference in imagery is apparent at almost any point of comparison, and it is perhaps best epitomized in the diverging descriptions of a debutante's coffee—

> From silver Spouts the grateful Liquors glide,
> While *China*'s Earth receives the smoking Tyde—
> (*Rape of the Lock*, III, 109–110)

and a bookseller's urine:

> . . . impetuous spread
> The stream, and smoking flourish'd o'er his head.
>
> (B, ii, 179–180)

But the differences in the narrative structure of the two poems, at first less conspicuous than metaphoric contrast, are equally important aspects of poetic meaning. Pope's conception of dulness grows into a complex vision of menacing inertia, and in his more somber conception the opposite of significant action is not insignificant action, as in the mock epic, but significant anti-action. To embody this vision he needed a new kind of narrative structure, and, with his characteristic talent for detecting satiric gold in contemporary lead, Pope saw such a structure near at hand. Implicit in the literary ideals and social behavior of the dunces Pope found a fable of duncery which could stand in exact opposition to epic.

The belief that the epic is didactic and essentially nationalistic was stated more or less strenuously by various Augustan students of the form. There seems to have been little difficulty in reconciling this doctrine with the idea of the epic's universality. John Dennis, for example, speaks easily of Virgil's "universal and Allegorical Action" while arguing in the same essay that Virgil's intention is also quite specific: "The Design that *Virgil* had in writing the *Æneis*, was to reconcile all the World, and more particularly the *Romans*, to the New Establishment, and the person of Augustus Caesar."[21] The core of Dennis's argument, now a cliché of literary criticism, is that great works are both timeless and timely, both universal and local in significance. It is not likely that Pope would have disagreed with his antagonist's assessment of the *Aeneid*; nor is it likely (so far as one can judge from Pope's notes to Homer) that he would have been troubled even by Blackmore's similar characterization of all epic poetry. Sir Richard had written that "Epick Poetry is indeed the Theology of the Country where the Poet lives . . . and a sort of Confession of the Publick Faith there established."[22] Pope must have granted

< EPIC INVERSION >

these premises more completely than either Dennis or Blackmore could have wished, for both men were to have memorable roles in his own "Confession of the Publick Faith" he saw permeating a dull, Hanoverian England. And he recognized the "Theology" of his country as one which elevated Dulness as its presiding deity. Blackmore's particular phrases, like his epic criticism in general, may help us feel the extent of Pope's alienation, for the "Publick Faith" and Pope's own beliefs are irreconcilable. Near the end of his life, Pope tried briefly to revive the epic posture, calling himself "My Countrys Poet" in the invocation of what was to have been an epic on the Trojan Brutus. He never got beyond that line.

However we may speculate about Pope's ability to deal with Britain's heroic legend, it seems clear that the gulf between his own cultural theology and the theology of his contemporary culture could be bridged only by the irony of inversion. Being as much in the Opposition as one can imagine, Pope could not write an epic about the duncical dismantling of a great island's civilization. For the same reason he could not write a mock epic about so solemn a subject. But he could and did write an anti-epic. He carefully structured his poem so that in the process of exhibiting none of the features of true epic it would exhibit all the features of his country's destructive Publick Faith. Because the logical inversion is so complete, the *Dunciad* extols amorality, passivity, and acquiescence as characteristic national "action"; lethargy, drowsiness, and, finally, everlasting sleep are its accomplishment. The inversion is even more striking when we recall Dennis's description of the *Aeneid* as a nationalistic poem. One feels, to borrow his language, that the ironic "Design" Pope had in writing the *Dunciad* "was to reconcile all the World," and "more particularly" the English, to "the New Establishment" of Dulness.

< CHAPTER THREE >

The Temple of Fame
and the "*Temple*
of Infamy"

The *Dunciad* received its title virtually by accident. Although Pope, in the personae of Martinus Scriblerus and Lewis Theobald, wrote elaborate "commentaries" on the title's derivation, orthography, and suitability, the mock-heroic name "Dunciad" was actually applied to the work at a rather late stage in its composition.[1] While Pope was at work on what now is the *Dunciad* it was rumored about London that he was tracing the "Progress of Dulness,"[2] and Pope himself privately referred to the poem as, simply, his "Dulness." In January of 1728 he told Swift, "It grieves me to the Soul that I cannot send you my Chef d'oeuvre, the Poem of Dulness, which after I am dead and gone, will be printed with a large Commentary, and letterd on the back, *Pope's Dulness*." One probably need look no further for an explanation of Pope's decision to change the title than the obvious fact that it would have been a liability to launch a controversial poem under the banner of "Dulness." A few weeks later he told Swift that his "Dulness" was to be known "for the future . . . by a more pompous name, The *Dunciad*."[3]

Amusing in its consequences, this sequence of authorial opinions reminds us that the *Dunciad* is dependent, first and last, upon an allegorical conception: Pope's "Poem of Dulness" is a

< TEMPLE OF FAME AND "TEMPLE OF INFAMY" >

poem about a personified, even mythologized abstraction. During the late seventeenth and early eighteenth centuries poems of this sort were often cast in one of two genres, the dream-vision or the progress piece. The latter form, deriving largely from the histori- cal self-consciousness which entered the literary imagination at the close of the Renaissance, was still relatively young when Pope began the *Dunciad*.[4] The dream-vision, on the other hand, was primarily a medieval genre, and it emerged quite frequently in the Augustan period in the specialized form of "temple" poems. One of the most accessible and fertile precedents, Chaucer's *Hous of Fame*, prompted Pope's youthful and brilliant imitation, the *Temple of Fame*. Pope at this point was following in the path of numerous other Augustan poets who had described the "temples" of numerous other abstractions. As allegorical visions the "temple" poem and the progress piece have many com- mon tendencies, and one can see their successful—perhaps inev- itable—fusion in the *Dunciad*.

1.

Pope may have completed his *Temple of Fame* as early as 1710, five years before its publication.[5] It is the work of a young man, but he did not lose interest in either the poem or its genre. In a note which he added to the *Dunciad* years later Pope referred to that poem in a way which intentionally recalled his Chaucerian venture of three decades past. A couplet from Book II of the 1728 *Dunciad*,

> Not Welsted so: drawn endlong by his scull,
> Furious he sinks; precipitately dull,
> (A, ii, 293–294)

had been changed in 1735 to read, "Not so bold Arnall . . . " By way of explaining Arnall's inclusion among the party writers Pope added the following note: "WILLIAM ARNALL, bred an Attorney, was a perfect Genius in this sort of work. . . . At the first publication of the Dunciad, he prevailed on the Author not

to give him his due place in it, by a letter professing his detesta-
tion of such practices as his Predecessor's. But since, by the most
unexampled insolence, and personal abuse of several great men,
the Poet's particular friends, he most amply deserved a niche in
the Temple of Infamy."[6] Like most of the notes to the *Dunciad*
this one is a mixture of humorous characterization and self-
justification; but the phrase "a niche in the Temple of Infamy"
is worth consideration. It may help us regard the poem as Pope
regarded it, for, in a fundamental sense, all the dunces were
deemed "most amply" deserving of just such a "niche" in a
larger design. It may also help us appreciate the justness of Pope's
prefatory claim that "whoever will consider the Unity of the
whole design, will be sensible, that the *Poem was not made for
these Authors, but these Authors for the Poem."*

Despite the burlesque and intentional insult, Pope reminds the
"Reader" of an all too easily forgotten truth: the poem does have
an independent unity, an integrity of its own, which is not seriously altered by the "inevitable removal of some Authors, and
insertion of others, in their Niches."[7] The niches of the *Dunciad*
are of course metaphorical rather than actual, but the principle
is similar to that of the *Temple of Fame* in that the specific persons are merely parts of a much larger edifice. Like the *Temple
of Fame*, the *Dunciad* is rooted more deeply in abstraction than
in fact, or, perhaps more accurately, the "facts" are collectively
subjected to an abstraction. Although it is true that much of
poetry is concerned with turning facts into something more significant, the *Temple of Fame* and the *Dunciad* occupy that particular province in which a poet seeks to organize certain historical
facts by means of a single allegorical principle.

That the details of the earlier poem are drawn from ancient
history and those of the *Dunciad* are culled from modern "history" is a difference which cannot (and is not intended to) be
ignored. For instance, Pope probably could not have written his
Temple of Fame without including Homer or Virgil. The "Temple of Infamy," however, might exist largely as it does without
Cibber or Theobald: neither is indispensable because Theobalds

< TEMPLE OF FAME AND "TEMPLE OF INFAMY" >

and Cibbers, after all, we have always with us. The very nature
of Pope's material and intention in the *Dunciad* dictates the
obvious difference in tone, since a poem recording the notorious
"fame" of characters so ephemeral they need footnotes can only
be written with pervasive irony. But this difference ought not to
obscure the *Dunciad*'s fundamental, if perverse, connection with
the *Temple of Fame*. From the early poetic experience of enshrin-
ing real figures in the niches of a temple to an abstraction Pope
learned a mode of poetry and perception which survived adaptation from the fame of the ancients to the infamy of the moderns.

2.

The *Temple of Fame* is not a "translation" but a free modern-
ization of those parts of Chaucer's *Hous of Fame* which Pope
found congenial. He drew primarily on the unfinished third book
of Chaucer's poem, expanding or editing with coherent intent
even where the parallels are most apparent, and his own prefatory
statement is a just description of the final result: "The Hint of
the following Piece was taken from *Chaucer's House of Fame*.
The Design is in a manner entirely alter'd, the Descriptions and
most of the particular Thoughts my own." It is necessary to realize just how different the poems are because either can suffer from
a too simplistic comparison. But it should be obvious that one
rarely turns to medieval and Augustan poetry for the same literary virtues. In accordance with his own principles of poetic
economy, Pope discards all of Chaucer's first book, and he uses
the second book primarily as the source for a few extended
similes. As Geoffrey Tillotson remarks, "The *Temple of Fame* is
everywhere cleared of the engaging 'Chaucerian' element of
pother and hotchpotch. . . . Chaucer's thousand spinning tetram-
eters are reduced to half the number of weighty pentameters.
For Chaucer's cinematographic speed and lightness there is
Pope's Handelian tempo and harmony, for Chaucer's narrative,
Pope's scene."[8]

The distinction between "Chaucer's narrative" and "Pope's

scene" is significant. For the "Design" is, as Pope claimed, "entirely altered," and the "manner" in which the alteration obtains has much to do with Pope's intention and poetic temperament. Chaucer used the structure of his *Hous of Fame* as he would later use the structure of the *Canterbury Tales*—that is, for its narrative possibilities. For example, in the first book, which describes the Temple of Venus, Chaucer rehearses the stories of the numerous and various women who were unfortunate in love. Dido, of course, is conspicuous there, since Venus

> . . . made Eneas so in grace
> Of Dido, quene of that contree,
> That, shortly for to tellen, she
> Becam hys love, and let him doo
> Al that weddynge longeth too,[9]

and there is even a litany of those good women whose legends cannot be conveniently included:

> Eke lo! how fals and reccheles
> Was to Breseyda Achilles,
> And Paris to Oenone;
> And Jason to Isiphile,
> And eft Jason to Medea;
> And Ercules to Dyanira,
> For he left hir for Yole,
> That made hym cache his deth, parde.
> (397–404)

Unlike Chaucer, however, Pope does not see himself as the chosen poet of love,[10] who is to be singled out by Jove's eagle because

> . . . thou so long trewely
> Hast served so ententyfly
> Hys blynde nevew Cupido,
> And faire Venus also.
> (615–618)

And since Pope does not choose to tell the stories of the lovelorn, he is free as well to eliminate Chaucer's garrulous eagle—that most philosophic of feathered bipeds—who conveys the poet from the Temple of Venus to the "paleys" of Fame.

< TEMPLE OF FAME AND "TEMPLE OF INFAMY" >

In place of this abundance of narrative and colloquial exchange, Pope concentrates in the first half of his poem on "painting" a few figures very carefully. In place of the "God's plenty"
of Chaucer's numerous heroes and heroines, all of whom have
their stories, Pope presents us with iconographic and statuesque
portraits of a few of culture's stony giants. The six pillars of his
intellectual pantheon support the figures of Homer, Pindar, Aristotle, Virgil, Horace, and Cicero—whom Pope refers to as "the
greatest Names in Learning of all Antiquity."[11] Partly because
Pope's conception of fame is closer, as A. C. Cawley has reminded
us,[12] to the Renaissance than to Chaucer (whose goddess evinces
her derivation from the Virgilian *Fama* or Rumor), his famous
men belong to a more "intellectual" world:

> A Train of Phantoms in wild Order rose,
> And, join'd, this Intellectual Scene compose.
>
> (9–10)

Pope's use of the adjective is probably not ours,[13] but the figures
who arrest his imagination are mainly those men who were felt
to have played a recognizable part in "learning." Of course Pope
is concerned with morality and utility as well as intellectuality,
and thus accords a place of honor to Confucius, "who taught
that useful Science to be *good*" (108). But one cannot imagine
Pope including

> The Ebrayk Josephus, the olde
> That of Jewes gestes tolde,
>
> (1433–1434)

whom Chaucer places "alderfirst" in his third book.

Yet Pope studies and expands Chaucer's descriptive mode even
when he is depicting classical rather than "gothic" figures. However alien Josephus, for example, may have been to his idea of
cultural greatness, Pope could find in the Chaucerian presenta-
tion of Josephus and a group of unnamed historians a useful
means of static, nondramatic representation:

> And he bar on hys shuldres hye
> The fame up of the Jewerye.

And by hym stoden other sevene,
Wise and worthy for to nevene,
To helpen him bere up the charge,
Hyt was so hevy and so large.
And for they writen of batayles,
As well as other olde mervayles,
Therfor was, loo, thys piler
Of which that I yow telle her,
Of led and yren bothe, ywys,
For yren Martes metal ys,
Which that god is of batayle;
And the led, withouten faille,
Ys, loo, the metal of Saturne,
That hath a ful large whel to turne.
(1435–1450)

Pope diverts such description from the subtleties of arcane lore and carries it toward emblematic representation, which relies more on visual elements such as facial expression and characteristic gesture. As the child of his age, he abandoned so medieval an iconography in favor of one which would be self-explanatory, if not transparent. In a more literary fashion he attempts to incorporate the significant emblems into the portraits themselves, and he even seeks an explicit correspondence between the style of his authorial characterizations and the style of the author's works. The main figures are described, Pope notes, "in such Attitudes as express their different Characters. The Columns on which they are rais'd are adorned with Sculptures, taken from the most striking Subjects of their Works; which Sculpture bears a Resemblance in its Manner and Character, to the Manner and Character of their Writings."[14] And, indeed, within the poem itself

Heroes in animated Marble frown,
And Legislators seem to think in Stone.
(73–74)

In his description of the pillar of Homer (whom Chaucer had mentioned only casually as one of the narrators of Troy's

< TEMPLE OF FAME AND "TEMPLE OF INFAMY" >

"fame")[15] Pope delineates more clearly the "animated Marble"
of his imagination:

> High on the first, the mighty *Homer* shone;
> Eternal Adamant compos'd his Throne;
> Father of Verse! in holy Fillets drest,
> His Silver Beard wav'd gently o'er his Breast;
> Tho' blind, a Boldness in his Looks appears,
> In Years he seem'd, but not impair'd by Years.
> The Wars of *Troy* were round the Pillar seen:
> Here fierce *Tydides* wounds the *Cyprian* Queen;
> Her *Hector* glorious from *Patroclus'* Fall,
> Here dragg'd in Triumph round the *Trojan* Wall.
> Motion and Life did ev'ry Part inspire,
> Bold was the Work, and prov'd the Master's Fire;
> A strong Expression most he seem'd t'affect,
> And here and there disclos'd a brave Neglect.
>
> (182–195)

This is not entirely successful as a portrait, for one may justly
wonder at Pope's own "strong Expression" which asks the reader
to visualize qualities beyond visualization, such as a "brave
Neglect" disclosing itself here and there. But the effort to trans-
late poetic character into poetic sculpture is apparent nonetheless. His description of Virgil is more successful in the terms of
its own emblematic language and stylistic iconography:

> A Golden Column next in Rank appear'd,
> On which a Shrine of purest Gold was rear'd;
> Finish'd the whole, and labour'd ev'ry Part,
> With patient Touches of unweary'd Art:
> The *Mantuan* there in sober Triumph sate,
> Compos'd his Posture, and his Look sedate;
> On *Homer* still he fix'd a reverend Eye,
> Great without Pride, in modest Majesty.
> In living Sculpture on the Sides were spread
> The *Latian* Wars, and haughty *Turnus* dead;
> *Eliza* stretch'd upon the fun'ral Pyre,
> *Æneas* bending with his aged Sire:
> *Troy* flam'd in burning Gold, and o'er the Throne
> *Arms and the Man* in Golden Cyphers shone.
>
> (196–209)

When Pope comes to describe Theobald years later (and Cibber still later) he calls upon a similar mode of pedestal sculpture to evoke expressive details. The passage at the opening of Book II of the *Dunciad*, which portrays Cibber "High on a gorgeous seat," begins as a rather close and avowed imitation of Milton. Where Satan had been described sitting "High on a throne of royal state,"[16] we see Cibber's elevation in allusive and ironic terms:

> High on a gorgeous seat, that far out-shone
> Henley's gilt tub, or Fleckno's Irish throne,
> Or that where on her Curls the Public pours,
> All-bounteous, fragrant Grains, and Golden show'rs,
> Great Cibber sate.   (B, ii, 1–5)

But then, in midline, the description broadens to incorporate both Miltonic allusion and the assumed poise of statuesque portraiture:

> . . . The proud Parnassian sneer,
> The conscious simper, and the jealous leer,
> Mix on his look: All eyes direct their rays
> On him, and crowds turn Coxcombs as they gaze.
> His Peers shine round him with reflected grace,
> New edge their dulness, and new bronze in their face.
> So from the Sun's broad beam, in shallow urns
> Heav'ns twinkling Sparks draw light, and point their horns.
>
>   (B, ii, 5–12)

Cibber is perfectly static, perfectly frozen at this point, immediately before the hectic activity of the second book gets underway. His "Peers"—who are both his duncical colleagues and "his" Lords—also stand in postured stillness, "reflecting" dulness like bronze statues, or perhaps like "Great Cibber's brazen, brainless brothers" in Book I. And a spiritual brother of Cibber's, a Renaissance dunce by the name of Querno[17] with whom the modern laureate is compared, is likewise depicted in monumental repose:

> Not with more glee, by hands Pontific crown'd,
> With scarlet hats wide-waving circled round,

< TEMPLE OF FAME AND "TEMPLE OF INFAMY" >

> Rome in her Capitol saw Querno sit,
> Thron'd on sev'n hills, the Antichrist of wit.
>
> (B, ii, 13–16)

Even when the "action" is apparently rapid Pope is perfectly capable of bringing it to a halt and painting a momentary tableau. I have noted earlier, for example, that Pope's description of the footrace between booksellers Lintot and Curll is virtually devoid of recognizable motion, as Pope carefully turns Miltonic imitation[18] to his own purpose:

> As when a dab-chick waddles thro' the copse
> On feet and wings, and flies, and wades, and hops;
> So lab'ring on, with shoulders, hands, and head,
> Wide as a wind-mill all his figures spread,
> With arms expanded Bernard rows his state,
> And left-legg'd Jacob seems to emulate.
>
> (B, ii, 63–68)

Jacob "seems to emulate" from the midst of this static description just as in the *Temple of Fame* "Legislators seem to think in Stone" (74) and Pindar "seem'd to labour with th' inspiring God" (213). Likewise Pope often uses a single, terse couplet to fix a character in a statuesque "attitude" in the dull heat of the activity of the games. One thinks of this description of a pseudonymous gazetteer,

> Fast by, like Niobe (her children gone)
> Sits Mother Osborne, stupify'd to stone!
>
> (B, ii, 311–312)[19]

or this of a miscellaneous author,

> In naked majesty Oldmixon stands,
> And Milo-like surveys his arms and hands.
>
> (B, ii, 283–284)[20]

In the *Temple of Fame* Pope depicts several authors as literally "supported" by their works: their statues, according to his note, rest on columns representing "their Writings." The description of a poet with whom Pope would identify so closely a few years later exemplifies this technique admirably:

> Here happy *Horace* tun'd th' *Ausonian* Lyre
> To sweeter Sounds, and temper'd *Pindar*'s Fire:
> Pleas'd with *Alcæus*' manly Rage t'infuse
> The softer Spirit of the *Sapphick* Muse.
> The polish'd Pillar diff'rent Sculptures grace;
> A Work outlasting Monumental Brass.
> Here smiling *Loves* and *Bacchanals* appear,
> The *Julian* Star, and Great *Augustus* here.
> The Doves that round the Infant Poet spread
> Myrtles and Bays, hung hov'ring o'er his Head.
>
> (222–231)

Though the enduring fame of a Horace may be justly supported by the productions of his well-tempered lyre, this metaphor undergoes a brazen alteration in the "Temple of Infamy." Various conspicuous writers and readers in the *Dunciad* are characterized by association with works they have produced or patronized —works, in other words, which have "supported" their pocketbooks or their notoriety, or both. The elaborate description of Cibber's "gothic" library (inherited from Theobald) is recalled at once, but an even closer metaphorical similarity can be seen in the brief description of "bold Benson" in Book IV. As a patron of means but not taste, William Benson had commissioned a Latin version of *Paradise Lost* (*mirabile scriptu*, one presumes) and had himself supervised three editions of a Scots physician's Latin psalms. In the *Dunciad* the appropriate miniature allegory of "support" is compressed into a single couplet:

> On two unequal crutches propt he came,
> Milton's on this, on that one Johnston's name.
>
> (IV, 111–112)

The same principle operates in the portrait of Italian Opera, who Pope envisions as "supported" by the debased taste of a decadent nobility:

> When lo! a Harlot form soft sliding by,
> With mincing step, small voice, and languid eye;
> Foreign her air, her robe's discordant pride
> In patch-work flutt'ring, and her head aside.

< TEMPLE OF FAME AND "TEMPLE OF INFAMY" >

By singing Peers up-held on either hand,
She tripp'd and laugh'd, too pretty much to stand.
(IV, 45–50)

The most interesting quality of each of these portraits is Pope's use of physical detail as an emblem of abstract qualities or (as in the couplet on Benson) complex and indicative circumstances. In part, the effect is analogous to the reductive humor of representing an intellectual process in baldly physical terms. Swift's version of Calvin as a petulant heir tearing his father's fabric and Pope's own fulsome dedicator who actually uses a quill to tickle patrons are two vivid instances of such a technique. The difference here is that Pope is concerned not with action in these particular portraits, but with qualities of personality and "properties" of existence which can be rendered in visual and static (or nearly static) terms. The descriptions of Cibber seated complacently in the midst of adulation, of Jacob "emulating" Curll, of Benson "propt" on Milton's name, and of Opera "up-held" by singing peers are all actually iconographic portraits which help establish a moral context. That is to say, they are static emblems such as Pope had first developed out of his adaptation of the more traditional and less self-contained iconography of Chaucer's significant "ymageries" (*Hous of Fame*, 1090).

Although portraits such as these constitute only a part of the *Dunciad*'s technical range, their iconographic quality is important as one of the forces which impel the *Dunciad* in a direction different from that of Pope's other satires. For normally when we think of Pope's satiric portraits we think first of the famous "character-sketches"[21] of Addison, who could

Damn with faint praise, assent with civil leer,
And without sneering, teach the rest to sneer;

or of one of those charming *exempla* who populate *Of the Characters of Women*:

Flavia's a Wit, has too much sense to Pray,
To Toast our wants and wishes, is her way;
Nor asks of God, but of her Stars to give

> The mighty blessing, "while we live, to live."
> Than all for Death, that Opiate of the soul!
> Lucretia's dagger, Rosamonda's bowl.
> Say, what can cause such impotence of mind?
> A Spark too fickle, or a Spouse too kind.
> Wise Wretch! with Pleasures too refin'd to please,
> With too much Spirit to be e'er at ease,
> With too much Quickness ever to be taught,
> With too much Thinking to have common Thought:
> Who purchase Pain with all that Joy can give,
> And die of nothing but a Rage to live.[22]

Pope's character sketches of this kind are brilliant and unsurpassed in their mixture of condemnation and compassion, but in the main they are not the sort of portraits that he uses in the *Dunciad*. There are few places in the *Dunciad* where Pope characterizes, as in the lines above, the subtle habits of speech and mind of an individual or a type character. Concerned less with the turns of thought and the eccentricities of motivation, the iconographic, emblematic portraits of the *Dunciad* are "portraits" in a more literal sense than the character sketches of the Horatian epistles. All of this affects our response throughout the poem as we begin to sense that the perspective which Pope establishes in the *Dunciad* is not that of an omniscient though colloquial man-about-town, but rather that of a keen and faithful observer of significant physical detail. Though in their own speeches the dunces reveal—in fact, proclaim—their mental habits and moral propensities quite directly, in the descriptions given by the poet himself such abstract qualities are suggested by means of indicative physical information.

The *Dunciad* has less worldly but more otherworldly wisdom than the Horatian poems, almost as if Pope had decided to compensate for the *Dunciad*'s tendency toward abstraction by emphasizing strongly the physical context of the dunces—their faces, their postures, their proper element, their chosen surroundings. But if this in any way approximates one's critical reaction to the poem, it probably does not adequately describe Pope's creative action in writing the *Dunciad*, for even so conscious a poet as

< TEMPLE OF FAME AND "TEMPLE OF INFAMY" >

Pope most likely thought less about "compensation" than about the mode of poetry proper for a very modern dream-vision. At any rate, such is the mode of description which Pope found in Chaucer's *Hous of Fame*:

> And next him on a piler stood
> Of soulfre, lyk as he were wood,
> Daun Claudian, the sothe to telle,
> That bar up al the fame of helle,
> Of Pluto, and of Prosperpyne,
> That quene ys of the derke pyne.
>
> (1507–1512)

Such, too, is the highly visual mode which he adapted for his own more Palladian *Temple of Fame*:

> Here in a Shrine that cast a dazling Light,
> Sate fix'd in Thought the mighty *Stagyrite*;
> His Sacred Head a radiant Zodiack crown'd,
> And various Animals his Sides surround;
> His piercing Eyes, erect, appear to view
> Superior Worlds, and look all Nature thro'.
>
> (232–237)

And such is the mode of emblematic description which Pope uses to portray diverse dunces in the appropriate niches of the "Temple of Infamy":

> Round him much Embryo, much Abortion lay,
> Much future Ode, and abdicated Play;
> Nonsense precipitate, like running Lead,
> That slip'd thro' Cracks and Zig-zags of the Head;
> All that on Folly Frenzy could beget,
> Fruits of dull Heat, and Sooterkins of Wit.
>
> (B, i, 121–126)

3.

Recognition of Pope's descriptive technique makes it possible to understand better his general intention in the *Dunciad*, for the poem is not a narrative poem except incidentally. The criticism of Mr. Sutherland, for example, that "few readers . . . have any clear picture of what is going on," does not really address the work Pope wrote. The *Dunciad* is primarily a descriptive poem dealing with the emblematic manifestations of an abstraction—Dulness. It is an allegorical vision, in other words, and to ask for a precise account of "what is going on" would be as inappropriate as a criticism contending that the *Temple of Fame* "lacks action."[23] Both poems have a slender thread of narrative which helps give them unity, but their essential "design" is the relation of a vision rather than the narration of a story.

When he published the *Temple of Fame* in 1715, Pope appended a prefatory note in which he attempted to defend allegory as a significant genre: "Some modern Criticks, from a pretended Refinement of Taste, have declar'd themselves unable to relish allegorical Poems. 'Tis not easy to penetrate into the meaning of this Criticism; for if *Fable* be allow'd one of the chief Beauties, or as *Aristotle* calls it, the very *Soul* of Poetry, 'tis hard to comprehend how that Fable should be less valuable for having a Moral." Despite the limitations inherent in Pope's stiffly conventional vocabulary, he appears to have been working toward a distinction between the function of "fable" in allegory and in straightforward narrative poetry: "We find an uncommon Charm in Truth, when it is convey'd by this Side-way to our Understanding; and 'tis observable, that even in the most ignorant Ages this way of Writing has found Reception. . . . Soon after *Chaucer* introduc'd it here, whose *Romaunt of the Rose, Court of Love, Flower and the Leaf, House of Fame,* and some others of his Writings are Masterpieces of this sort. In Epick Poetry, 'tis true, too nice and exact a Pursuit of the Allegory is justly esteem'd a Fault; and *Chaucer* had the Discernment to avoid it in his *Knight's Tale,* which was an attempt towards an Epick Poem." This comment deserves closer scrutiny than it has received. It is a way of saying that allegory might legitimately be loose in narrative because "this Side-way to our Understanding" depends more heavily upon description. It is significant that in later editions Pope abandoned this obviously ill-suited, pseudo-

< TEMPLE OF FAME AND "TEMPLE OF INFAMY" >

Aristotelian justification of an unclassical poetic form and re-
placed it with a shorter statement of intent and precedent: "This
poem is introduced in the manner of the *Provencial* Poets, whose
works were for the most part Visions, or pieces of imagination,
and constantly descriptive."[24]

The awkward term "fable" has disappeared to be supplanted
by "Visions," "pieces of imagination," and the suggestive phrase
"constantly descriptive." Pope was not one to make even minor
editorial changes without consideration ("Among the poets, Pope
is the great editor," a recent student of his revisions has said)[25]
and by 1736 he must have sensed more acutely that the *Temple
of Fame* contains many striking features of the dream-vision
which could hardly be explained in terms borrowed from epic
criticism. The relation could only be tenuous, for example,
between the Augustan notion of "fable" or "action"[26] and this
emblematic description of the northern front of Fame's temple:

> Of *Gothic* structure was the Northern Side,
> O'er-wrought with Ornaments of barb'rous Pride.
> There huge Colosses rose, with Trophies crown'd,
> And *Runic* Characters were grav'd around:
> There sate *Zamolxis* with erected Eyes,
> And *Odin* here in mimick Trances dies.
> There, on rude Iron Columns smear'd with Blood,
> The horrid Forms of *Scythian* Heroes stood,
> *Druids* and *Bards* (their once loud Harps unstrung)
> And Youths that dy'd to be by Poets sung.
> These and a Thousand more of doubtful Fame,
> To whom old Fables gave a lasting Name,
> In Ranks adorn'd the Temple's outward Face;
> The Wall in lustre and Effect like Glass,
> Which o'er each Object casting various Dies,
> Enlarges some, and others multiplies.
> Nor void of Emblem was the mystic Wall,
> For thus Romantick Fame increases all.

(119–136)

Pope's attitude toward Northern valor is derived directly from
Sir William Temple,[27] but what concerns us here is the manner

of allegorizing this visual context. The "moral" of distortion in the concluding lines bears a striking resemblance to the similarly moralized description in the *Dunciad* of Dulness surveying the literary miscreations she had inspired:

> All these, and more, the cloud-compelling Queen
> Beholds thro' fogs, that magnify the scene.
> She, tinsel'd o'er in robes of varying hues,
> With self-applause her wild creation views;
> Sees momentary monsters rise and fall,
> And with her own fools-colours gilds them all.
>
> (B, i, 79–84)

And in a passage from near the end of the fourth book—a passage neither unrelated "Nor void of Emblem"—Pope uses telling physical description to suggest the vagaries of obscured vision:

> On others Int'rest her gay liv'ry flings,
> Int'rest, that waves on Party-colour'd wings:
> Turn'd to the Sun, she casts a thousand dyes,
> And, as she turns, the colours fall or rise.
>
> (IV, 537–540)

The impulse at work in each of the passages above is certainly not narrative: the passages are parts, in Pope's words, of "Visions, or pieces of imagination, and constantly descriptive." This mode of poetry held a strong attraction for Pope, and it is perhaps not surprising that one should find him discussing the aesthetics of "Vision" poetry eight years after the *Temple of Fame* had been published and five years before the *Dunciad* would make its first appearance.

In the year 1723 Pope was literally in the middle of his long engagement with Homer. His translation of the *Iliad* had been published and the first part of the *Odyssey* was two years away. In the early autumn of that year he wrote a thoughtful letter to Judith Cowper concerning not Homer, but the nature of poetry written "in the descriptive way":

This beautiful season will raise up so many Rural Images & Descriptions in a Poetical Mind that I expect You & all such as

< TEMPLE OF FAME AND "TEMPLE OF INFAMY" >

you (if there be any such), at least all who are not Downright dull Translators like your Servant, must necessarily be productive of Verses. . . . I could wish you tryd something in the descriptive way on any Subject you please, mixd with Vision & Moral; like the Pieces of the old Provençal Poets, which abound with Fancy & are the most amusing scenes in nature. There are 3 or 4 of this kind in Chaucer admirable.

The tone is wistful, and as one of humankind Pope was perfectly capable of urging upon a friend a project which he longed to pursue himself. In the same letter he says:

I have long had an inclination to tell a Fairy tale; the more wild & exotic the better, therefore a *Vision*, which is confined to no rules of probability, will take in all the Variety & luxuriancy of Description you will. Provided there be an apparent moral to it. I think one or 2 of the Persian Tales would give one Hints for such an Invention: And perhaps if the Scenes were taken from Real places that are known, in order to compliment particular Gardens & Buildings of a fine taste, (as I believe several of Chaucer's descriptions do, tho tis what nobody has observed) it would add great beauty to the whole.—I wish you found such an amusement pleasing to you; If you did but, at leisure, form descriptions from Objects in nature itself which struck you most livelily, I would undertake to find a Tale that shoud bring em all together: which you'l think an odd undertaking, but in a Piece of this fanciful & Imaginary nature I am sure is practicable.[28]

This long letter reveals much about the interests and inclinations of a poet whom many readers still regard almost exclusively as the man who brought Homer, Horace, and Arabella Fermor into the mainstream of English poetry. One sees here another side of Pope, an element of his personality which shows clearly that the imitation of Chaucer was more than a youthful exercise.[29] In a more technical way, the letter is interesting for what it indicates about Pope's view of descriptive poetry "mixd with Vision & Moral." His projected "Fairy Tale" or "Vision" would be "confined to no rules of probability" because its narrative structure would be unimportant. His offer to provide a tale which would bring Miss Cowper's descriptive passages "all together" underscores his belief that narrative is rather an afterthought in a "Piece of this fanciful & Imaginary nature." Significant too is Pope's suggestion that the descriptions be based on "Real places that are known"—as he conjectures Chaucer's were—so that the writer might "compliment particular Gardens and Buildings of a fine Taste."

After the *Temple of Fame*, Pope did not write the "wild & exotic" poem of the sort described to Judith Cowper and for which he "long had an inclination." But definite features of this project of the early 1720s make themselves felt in the long ironic poem which he probably began to write within two or three years of this letter.[30] In the *Dunciad* there is a stronger emphasis on description or "scene" (to use the word which Pope and Mr. Tillotson employ) than on narrative coherence. There is the *Dunciad*'s delightful and effective "improbability"—a quality which John Dennis sought to discredit with heavy-handed scorn by declaring that the games of Book II could never have taken place in "the Master Street of a populous City."[31] There is the constant mixture throughout of "Vision & Moral" in the descriptive passages.

Other qualities appear as they are transformed by the *Dunciad*'s comprehensive irony, for the relation between Pope's remarks to Judith Cowper and the *Dunciad* itself is like the inverted correspondence between conventional pastoral theory and Gay's "Newgate pastoral."[32] The *Dunciad* is an urban fairy tale, a Grub Street dream-vision that eventually assumes the proportions of a nightmare. In place of the "many Rural Images," which Pope had in mind earlier, there are the City scenes of "Fleet-ditch with disemboguing streams," and the unbucolic "Cave of Poverty and Poetry." In place of the "Scenes taken from Real places that are known," which would commend monuments of "fine Taste," there are the descriptions of urban monstrosities such as Bethlehem Hospital "where Folly holds her throne" and

> Where o'er the gates, by his fam'd father's hand
> Great Cibber's brazen, brainless brothers stand,

< TEMPLE OF FAME AND "TEMPLE OF INFAMY" >

or emblems of supremely bad taste such as "Curl's chaste press, and Lintot's rubric post."

It is as if Pope's plan for a pleasant, even idyllic "Vision" soured between 1723 and 1728, while the impetus to explore further the conventions of the dream-vision remained to find expression in an ironic vision of a very tawdry metropolis. The inversion is thoroughgoing because it derives from Pope's fundamental equation of the goddess Dulness with "infamy," with the opposite of the deity who presided over his earlier, more conventional dream-vision, the *Temple of Fame*. I do not mean merely that Pope spoke of the *Dunciad* as the "Temple of Infamy" in a footnote—although this in itself is significant—but that he had good reason for doing so. The inversion, in other words, is inherent in Pope's conception of his subject. For Pope, as for us, "fame" means "good reputation"; but he sees the "never-blushing"[33] sons of Dulness as men eager to achieve any reputation by any means—an ethic analogous to the contemporary public relations principle that any publicity is good publicity.

While the association of Dulness and Infamy is implicit throughout the poem in the behavior of the votaries of the goddess—primarily because they are unabashed votaries—this equation becomes most explicit near the end of the fourth book when the "Magus" performs an important function on behalf of Dulness. The magician figure may come from Garth's *Dispensary* or from Fielding's *Vernoniad*, but in the *Dunciad* he is transmuted into a more complex force.[34] As an amalgamation of Walpole and Circe, the

> . . . WIZARD OLD his *Cup* extends;
> Which whoso tastes, forgets his former friends,
> Sire, Ancestors, Himself. One casts his eyes
> Up to a *Star*, and like Endymion dies:
> A *Feather* shooting from another's head
> Extracts his brain, and Principle is fled,
> Lost is his God, his Country, ev'ry thing;
> And nothing left but Homage to a King!
> The vulgar herd turn off to roll with Hogs,
> To run with Horses, or to hunt with Dogs;

> But, sad example! never to escape
> Their Infamy, still keep the human shape.
>
> (IV, 517–528)

And the tragedy of it all is that Infamy carries within itself the sorry solace of self-deception. The dunces do not even regret the obliteration of Fame's potentially ennobling call, because Dulness keeps them far from the truth:

> But she, good Goddess, sent to ev'ry child
> Firm Impudence, or Stupefaction mild;
> And strait succeeded, leaving shame no room,
> Cibberian forehead, or Cimmerian gloom.
> Kind Self-conceit to some her glass applies,
> Which no one looks in with another's eyes:
> But as the Flatt'rer or Dependant paint,
> Beholds himself a Patriot, Chief, or Saint.
> On others Int'rest her gay liv'ry flings,
> Int'rest, that waves on Party-colour'd wings:
> Turn'd to the Sun, she casts a thousand dyes,
> And, as she turns, the colours fall or rise.
> Others the Syren Sisters warble round,
> And empty heads console with empty sound.
> No more, alas! the voice of Fame they hear,
> The balm of Dulness trickling in their ear.
>
> (IV, 529–544)

The power of Dulness, whether ministered by the goddess herself or by her "Magus," operates in direct opposition to the motivation of Fame. Pope's assertion at this late point in the final book of the *Dunciad* does not come as a sudden revelation. Arriving at this passage we recall that at the beginning of the fourth book Dulness had already enchained "sober History," the embodiment of genuine and lasting reputation, who nonetheless

> . . . restrain'd her rage,
> And promis'd Vengeance on a barb'rous age.
>
> (IV, 39–40)

We assume that History is in bondage because she is not permitted by the times to record the deeds of greatness, and later in the

< TEMPLE OF FAME AND "TEMPLE OF INFAMY" >

book Dulness urges her votaries to block further Fame's remaining avenue—legitimate literary reputation:

> "Leave not a foot of verse, a foot of stone,
> A Page, a Grave, that they can call their own;
> But spread, my sons, your glory thin or thick,
> On passive paper, or on solid brick.
> So by each Bard an Alderman shall sit,
> A heavy Lord shall hang at ev'ry Wit,
> And while on Fame's triumphal Car they ride,
> Some Slave of mine be pinion'd to their side."
>
> (IV, 127–134)

And when the Grand Tourist returns from his disastrous year on the Continent, having "Spoil'd his own language, and acquir'd no more," he and his dubious mistress are likewise confirmed by Dulness in their opposition to worthwhile reputation:

> Pleas'd, she accepts the Hero, and the Dame,
> Wraps in her Veil, and frees from sense of Shame.
>
> (IV, 335–336)

Accordingly it is in her capacity as progenitor of blindness and self-deception that Dulness is addressed still later (IV, 470) as the "Mother of Arrogance, and source of Pride!" The stage is now well prepared for the more emphatic association of Dulness and Infamy which we witness near the conclusion of the *Dunciad*.

4.

The fourth book of the *Dunciad* has attracted as much commentary in recent years as the rest of the poem, and not all of its discussion has been limited to the moral and intellectual "issues" of this book.[35] Its formal structure, in particular, has been the subject of two provocative essays; George Sherburn's "The *Dunciad*, Book IV" and Aubrey Williams's study of the "Literary Backgrounds to Book Four of the *Dunciad*" are attempts to define and explain the structure Pope employs. In brief, Mr. Sherburn regards Book IV as a "grand drawing-room" scene, and he argues that Pope was probably influenced by various farces written by Fielding in the 1730s, theatrical pieces which "had shown royal levees crammed with incongruous episodes that followed each other kaleidoscopically much as do the passages of Book IV." Mr. Williams agrees basically with this account, but he also sees in Book IV Pope's reliance upon the "Triumph" genre, a "familiar allegorical convention deriving from an anonymous and pre-Christian work called the *Tablet of Cebes (Cebestis Tabula)*," and, more immediately, the influence of several Augustan poems in which a "session" of writers or performers contend for the notice of a presiding deity. Rochester's *Session of the Poets* is one of the more familiar examples, but the satiric type goes back at least to Suckling.[36]

Although both of these studies attest to the fascinating appeal of the fourth book's "dreamlike"[37] unreality, it seems to me that neither sufficiently takes into account the "influence" of Pope's personal past and his own experimentation with the poetry of dream-vision. For, considered structurally, Book IV is actually an ironic, elaborately inverted version of the grand convocation in the *Temple of Fame*. I am not attempting to reduce the fourth book to an imitation—which, even in the less pejorative Augustan sense of the word, it is not—or to deny that Pope's readers may have been better prepared to accept the book as a result of their familiarity with "session" satires or Fieldingesque farces. Still, the evidence in the poetry itself for these influences is not particularly convincing, and it should be remembered that neither the burlesque "session" poem nor the theatrical farce would have provided a natural vehicle for the high-toned mixture of "Vision & Moral" which permeates Book IV. On the other hand, critical consideration of portions of the *Temple of Fame* and the last book of the "Temple of Infamy" may illuminate the range of Pope's irony and define the mode in which he sought to complete adequately the structure he had begun fifteen years earlier.

The second part of the *Temple of Fame* begins with the call of Fame's trumpet, a clarion which summons "promiscuous

< TEMPLE OF FAME AND "TEMPLE OF INFAMY" >

Throngs" of petitioners to her throne—"For Good and Bad alike are fond of Fame" (293). At this point the poem becomes dramatic as well as descriptive:

> Around these Wonders as I cast a Look,
> The Trumpet sounded, and the Temple shook,
> And all the Nations, summon'd at the Call,
> From diff'rent Quarters fill the crowded Hall:
> Of various Tongues the mingled Sounds were heard;
> In various Garbs promiscuous Throngs appear'd;
> Thick as the Bees, that with the Spring renew
> Their flow'ry Toils, and sip the fragrant Dew,
> When the wing'd Colonies first tempt the Sky,
> O'er dusky Fields and shaded Waters fly,
> Or settling, seize the Sweets the Blossoms yield,
> And a low Murmur runs along the Field.
> Millions of suppliant Crowds the Shrine attend,
> And all Degrees before the Goddess bend;
> The Poor, the Rich, the Valiant, and the Sage,
> And boasting Youth, and Narrative old Age.
>
> (276–291)

We have seen this same "promiscuous" blurring of distinctions— "all Degrees before the Goddess bend"—throughout the *Dunciad*, and in Book IV the process occurs in a similarly dramatic situation when "Fame's posterior Trumpet" (IV, 70) sounds *its* call. By this "posterior" fame Pope means to express the opposite of desirable reputation—in a word, infamy. One critic has unfortunately used this passage to demonstrate Pope's lifelong faith in worldly reputation as an incentive to virtue;[38] the incentive here, however, is obviously not fame. But it is all one to the votaries of Dulness, and the trumpet marks the beginning of Book IV's action:

> And now had Fame's posterior Trumpet blown,
> And all the Nations summon'd to the Throne.
> The young, the old, who feel her inward sway,
> One instinct seizes, and transports away.
> None need a guide, by sure Attraction led,
> And strong impulsive gravity of Head:
> None want a place, for all their Centre found,

> Hung to the Goddess, and coher'd around.
> Not closer, orb in orb, conglob'd are seen
> The buzzing Bees about their dusky Queen.
>
> (IV, 71–80)

It is not surprising that the last line recalls the metaphorical crowding "thick as the Bees" from the *Temple of Fame* (as well as from Virgil and Milton), nor that the "bees" in the *Dunciad* are only part of a larger metaphor which turns, "orb in orb," into the grand "Vortex" of Dulness a few lines later. For the *Dunciad* is a much more complex poem than the *Temple of Fame*, a much better poem in that even its conventional similes are typically parts of coherent and elemental patterns of imagery. But the real similarity of the poems at this point lies in their conceptual affinity: a large parade of votaries is led, on signal and by "sure Attraction," to the throne of the deity who has governed their lives. Despite the antithetical natures of Fame and Dulness, the goddesses' respective trumpets mark the beginning of imaginary Last Judgments in which all followers successively assert their own merits and claim their rewards.

An overview of what follows from this point in the two poems reveals further similarities. In the *Temple of Fame* the goddess hears the petitions of eight separate groups of supplicants. Although less capricious than Chaucer's Fame,[39] she still has "fickle Fortune" (296) for a sister, and consequently she rewards and punishes with little justice or even consistency:

> Some she disgrac'd, and some with Honours crown'd;
> Unlike Successes equal Merits found.
>
> (294–295)

The order of these petitioners is as follows: (1) the "Learned World," whose diligence Fame rewards with renown (298ff); (2) the "Good and Just, and awful Train," also granted Fame (318ff); (3) a similar and equally deserving "Band," whom the goddess denies the "Golden Trumpet of eternal Praise" and damns instead with the "black Trumpet" of "dire Report" (328ff); (4) a group of conquering soldiers, whose deeds Fame

< TEMPLE OF FAME AND "TEMPLE OF INFAMY" >

"in dark Oblivion drown'd" (342ff); (5) a group of virtuous recluses who ask simply to "die unheard of, as we liv'd unseen," but who become famous nevertheless (356ff); (6) a "Train" of rakes and fops who ask, and receive, reputation for amatory conquests never made (378ff); (7) a similar group, whom Fame derides (394ff); (8) a "gloomy Tribe" of Machiavellian villains who "boast of mighty Mischiefs done" and whom the "dread Sound" of infamy rewards (406ff).

All of this is remarkably like the pageant of petitioners in Book IV of the *Dunciad*. There are differences, of course. For one thing, Dulness is terribly consistent in dealing with *her* votaries—rewarding even the "vast involuntary Throng"!—and she therefore deals out "their Infamy" collectively rather than individually (IV, 527ff). In the *Dunciad*, furthermore, Pope achieves greater verisimilitude by allowing only one votary to speak at a time, instead of in chorus. But various individuals merely speak for various groups of like-minded colleagues: Dr. Busby, for example, is the representative of mindless education, and Bentley of mindless learning. There are eight such groups, as it turns out, who make their way to the throne of Dulness. The numerical coincidence is probably just that, and it is not possible to make exact connections between the groups in the *Temple of Fame* and those in the "Temple of Infamy." But it seems Pope did intend to re-create near the end of each poem an allegorical scene of essentially the same proportions.

Just as there is at first a great press around the throne of Fame, when "Millions of suppliant Crowds the Shrine attend" (288), so there is thronging confusion beneath the throne of Dulness:

> Now crowds on crowds around the Goddess press,
> Each eager to present the first Address.
> Dunce scorning Dunce beholds the next advance,
> But Fop shews Fop superior complaisance.
> (IV, 135–138)

Then the scene clears somewhat (also as in the *Temple of Fame*), and the several groups of claimants or their representatives appear in this order: (1) Dr. Busby, who had already attained near-mythic stature as the "Spectre" of repressive education (139ff); (2) Bentley, who emerges from the midst of "a hundred head of Aristotle's friends," representing the worst tendencies of Scholasticism (189ff); (3) a "gay embroider'd race" of fops, represented at large by the "Attendant Orator" and the conspicuous achievements of his Grand Tourist (275ff); (4) a "lazy, lolling sort . . . of ever-listless Loit'rers" (337ff); (5) Annius and Mummius (whom we instinctively regard, like Rosencrantz and Guildenstern, as one person) representing dull, even vicious antiquarians (347ff);[40] (6) a "tribe, with weeds and shells fantastic crown'd," whose pursuits are exemplified in the ensuing argument between a butterfly-bewitched entomologist and a carnation-charmed botanist (397ff); (7) the "gloomy Clerk," an atheist who "damns implicit faith" though he himself is "prompt to impose, and fond to dogmatize" (459ff); (8) Silenus, the "bowzy Sire" who typifies the modern, self-deceiving, depraved variety of Epicureanism (493ff).

This elaborate convocation of the votaries of Dulness provides a means of exemplifying and defining dramatically the abstraction which is the real subject of Pope's poem—Dulness herself. In its barest terms an abstraction is only an intellectual convenience, a way of explaining or classifying various facts which appear to have common features or which seem somehow to belong to the same denomination. Philosophical temperament, of course, may determine whether one man habitually regards empirical "evidence" or intuitive "Ideas" as the true "facts of life," but a poet writing about an abstraction has to accommodate both. He must illustrate abstraction by instance and incident. Throughout the *Dunciad* the dunces are enlisted—either by actual names like Curll or generic names like Annius—in the service of exemplification. In Pope's design the numerous votaries help to make Dulness visible, revealing the force and extent of her otherwise invisible "sway," much as smoke shows the direction of the wind. Personification is in itself part of the poet's intention to make the abstraction "real" for the reader, but the mere transformation of dulness to Dulness, of neuter gender to feminine, is not enough, and Pope therefore portrays the goddess Dulness by describing her far-reaching effects upon "real" men. Moreover, the process is reciprocal: the dunces are characterized, at least in part, by their association with Dulness and their devotion to her. It is a very simple design, but what is striking is Pope's ability to maintain a constant level of abstraction in the course of a poem so heavily laden with allusions to specific facts, names, and incidents; for the particular dunces are ultimately important only insofar as their presence testifies to the validity and credibility of the poet's abstract conception.

The structure of the fourth book, with its close resemblance to the masquelike structure of Pope's earlier poem about an abstraction—the *Temple of Fame*—is the final exposition of the power of Dulness, the grotesque and ludicrous counterpart of Fame. It is an extended exemplification of that "sure Attraction" which exerts its final pull at the sounding of "Fame's posterior Trumpet," the abstract call of Dulness to "the young, the old, who feel her inward sway," and whom "one instinct seizes, and transports away." The significant similarities between the fourth book and the *Temple of Fame* stem from their common conception, for in each place Pope is concerned with an abstract principle which comes to underlie and integrate the poet's vision of civilization. In both works the abstraction is measured and "proven" by describing the sorts of men who might address their goddess, either in word or deed, as unreservedly as the "attendant Orator" addresses Dulness: "Thou, only thou, directing all our way!" (IV, 296). As in the *Temple of Fame*, the convocation structure allows Pope to dramatize the essential like-mindedness operating in ostensibly different types of men. In the *Temple of Fame* scholars, soldiers, fops, and tyrants all come before the same throne, just as in the *Dunciad* the "gay embroider'd race," the pedants, the dilettantes, and the freethinkers all throng to the throne of Dulness.

Most readers of the *Dunciad* have been willing to grant the fourth book a rather high level of abstraction. Even so unsympathetic a commentator as Gilbert Highet finds it more "impersonal" and "healthy" than the rest of the poem.[41] But Book IV merely completes the design of the earlier books. For one thing, the idea at the root of the entire poem's metaphorical scheme—the idea that the dissolution of generic distinctions constitutes uncreation—marches to its logical conclusion in Book IV as "bard and blockhead" march toward chaos "side by side" (IV, 101). It is equally important, however, to notice that the fourth book's allegorical, "Temple-of-Fame" structure is mirrored too, though less distinctly, in much of the supposedly "personal" *Dunciad*, particularly in the shifting contests and pageantry of the second and third books.

Book II has been alternately praised for its observance of mock-epic decorum and damned for its "mean" subject matter.[42] The former opinion is based on Pope's obvious and successful burlesque imitation of the funeral games in the *Iliad* and *Aeneid*, while the latter judgment is a reaction to his use of real names and real filth. But, favorable or unfavorable, both estimates are myopic in that they overemphasize the particular fact of the parodic games themselves (the footraces and diving contests) and virtually ignore the more general movement and tenor of Book II as a whole. Certainly the reader is expected to remember Homer and Virgil, and certainly he is expected to realize that unscrupulous booksellers and writers deal in "dirt." But by using a crowded, generalized scene and various scene changes similar to those employed in the *Temple of Fame* Pope also asks the reader to be alive to the abstract principle of Infamy or Dulness as it is represented by the numerous votaries who come forward when their goddess summons "all her Race" (B, ii, 19). For Book II is much broader in scope than its incidental ridicule of Curll or Lintot or Blackmore, because the "Race" of Dulness is actually a vast "endless band" which is drawn from "half the land" (B, ii, 19–20). Included in its numbers are

> All who true Dunces in her cause appear'd,
> And all who knew those Dunces to reward.
>
> (B, ii, 25–26)

This is not simply humorous hyperbole. Although the second book has a few particular "stars," Pope repeatedly suggests that they have been literally singled out "from the Herd"[43] (just as in Book IV Bentley or Busby represents a herd of similar disciples); and at several points participants emerge into view from the midst of a nearly anonymous crowd. In particular, the transitions of Book II closely resemble the rapid, crowded shifts of the *Temple of Fame*. In place of a sudden stage direction which unexpectedly introduces a new group of Fame's votaries—

> This Band dismiss'd, behold another Crowd
> Prefer'd the same Request
>   (328–329)

—the reader may find a similarly quick movement in the *Dunciad* from one group of participants to another:

> But now for Authors nobler palms remain;
> Room for my Lord!   (B, ii, 191–192)

These transitions are abruptly imperative, even fragmented, and they are designed to intensify the effect of universal crowding and the vastness of the stage. The same principle operates in various passages from both poems, as new "bands" strive to be noticed by their goddesses:

> Pleas'd with the strange Success, vast Numbers prest
> Around the Shrine, and made the same Request.
>   (394–395)

> Now thousand tongues are heard in one loud din:
> The Monkey-mimics rush discordant in.
>   (B, ii, 235–236)

We also find similar descriptions of professional falsifiers in the two poems. This passage from the *Temple of Fame* introduces various charlatans who deal in "rumor":

> Above, below, without, within, around,
> Confus'd, unnumber'd Multitudes are found,

95

> Who pass, repass, advance, and glide away;
> Hosts rais'd by Fear, and Phantoms of a Day.
>
> (458–461)

These lines from the *Dunciad* describe those modern-day rumor-mongers, the gazetteers, in the employ of Dulness:

> Next plung'd a feeble, but a desp'rate pack,
> With each a sickly brother at his back:
> Sons of a Day!   (B, ii, 305–307)

Looking beyond the mock-heroic contests one can see that Book II actually points more clearly toward the dream world of the fourth book of the *Dunciad*—also a broad "vision" ending in sleep—than to Virgil's narration of physical contests. Both books grow out of Pope's early assimilation of the Chaucerian dream-vision mode, and Book II stands, in conception as well as composition, midway between the *Temple of Fame* and the final surrealistic vision of the "New Dunciad." In each vision the scene is overwhelmed by homogeneous crowds. In the *Temple of Fame* a "train" of rakes come before their goddess:

> Next these a youthful Train their Vows exprest,
> With Feathers crown'd, with gay Embroid'ry drest;
> Hither, they cry'd, direct your Eyes, and see
> The Men of Pleasure, Dress, and Gallantry.
>
> (378–381)

Their "educated" equivalents, the intellectual fops, trip onto the stage in Book II of the *Dunciad*:

> Three College Sophs, and three pert Templars came,
> The same their talents, and their tastes the same;
> Each prompt to query, answer, and debate,
> And smit with love of Poesy and Prate.
>
> (B, ii, 379–382)

Finally, in the fourth book, enter a similar "race" of votaries who have been debauched in both body and mind:

> In flow'd at once a gay embroider'd race,
> And titt'ring push'd the Pedants off the place:

< TEMPLE OF FAME AND "TEMPLE OF INFAMY" >

Some would have spoken, but the voice was drown'd
By the French horn, or by the op'ning hound.
(IV, 275–278)

The passages are nearly interchangeable, and they exemplify resemblances which are at once thematic and structural. In the *Temple of Fame* Pope uses rapid, extravagant transitions to suggest a large and crowded scene populated by various groups of essentially like-minded votaries. In the "Temple of Infamy" the same intention, complicated by the irony of inversion, embraces a larger and larger portion of humankind:

Each Songster, Riddler, ev'ry nameless name,
All crowd, who foremost shall be damn'd to Fame.
(B, iii, 157–158)

The names in the *Dunciad* are ultimately "nameless" because the particular dunces are merely manifestations of Dulness. This is not to deny the "personal" aspect of the poem or, for that matter, the enjoyment which Pope and most of his readers derived from the use of recognizable names. But the impersonality of the *Dunciad* should not be ignored. By insistently subordinating the dunces to a mode of emblematic description and a poetic structure appropriate for a "vision" of an abstraction, Pope continually invites the reader to look past the individuals to the goddess directing all their way. The structure, in particular, of the second and fourth books enables Pope to attain the same level of abstraction he had attained (with much more "poetic" material) in the *Temple of Fame*. In the first and third books Pope relies less directly on the devices of the "temple" genre, using instead aspects of another kind of allegorical poem, the "progress piece." We shall see, however, that these two types of poetry about personified abstractions are finally one in the poetry of Pope.

5.

Whether or not Pope himself seriously considered calling the *Dunciad* the "Progress of Dulness," we know that many of his contemporaries believed the rumored title appropriate,[44] for the poem's Augustan readers would have been quick to appreciate Pope's use of various conventions associated with the progress piece. The progress piece was a popular minor genre throughout much of the seventeenth and all of the eighteenth century, and R. H. Griffith has defined it as a poem describing the "imaginary tour of an allegorical abstraction."[45] Denham's *Progress of Learning* (1668) and Gray's *Progress of Poesy* (1757) are two of the better known (and better) examples of the type. Denham's poem, for instance, traces what we might now call the "development" of acquired knowledge as it passed from Eden to Egypt, Greece, Rome, and Western Europe. The *Progress of Poesy*, though a more complex poem, follows more or less the same outline.

The word "progress" considered carefully is in itself an indication of the genre's combination of physical and abstract elements. In the seventeenth and eighteenth centuries the word had already partly assumed the evaluative, self-congratulatory meaning it now has, and it is hardly accidental that many "progress" poems are panegyrics (for example, Dryden's *To Sir Godfrey Kneller*; *To My Honor'd Friend, Dr. Charleton*; Lansdowne's *Progress of Beauty*; Carew's *Elegie upon the Death of the Deane of Pauls, Dr. John Donne*). But the word also retained its older, descriptive meaning of a pageant or formal procession. By working with both meanings a poet could readily allegorize, say, cultural history in terms of a grand intellectual parade and thus describe a credible "imaginary tour of an allegorical abstraction." Or the poet might attempt to endow an actual, physical "progress" with symbolic significance, as Thomas Tickell did when he enthusiastically described the *Royal Progress* in 1714. (Neither Tickell nor George I were great enough to convince us that the Hanoverian journey to England constituted the progress of virtue, but Tickell plainly intended just such an allegorization.) I wish to consider the progress piece more critically, but one can discern at this point that Pope has the double meaning of progress very much in mind when he describes the movement of the dunces from the City to the Court. Instead of the "Progress of Learn-

< TEMPLE OF FAME AND "TEMPLE OF INFAMY" >

ing," the procession of duncery represents a "Progress of Dulness."

Many of the so-called progress poems of the seventeenth and eighteenth centuries actually have little to do with progress as a cultural phenomenon, and it is the cultural progress piece—with its conventions of history, prophecy, and praise—that concerns us here. Numerous poems with "progress" in their titles, such as Swift's satiric *Progress of Beauty* or Prior's burlesque *Alma: or, The Progress of Mind,* have virtually nothing in common with poems like those of Denham and Gray mentioned earlier. On the other hand, several poems whose titles do not employ the word "progress" are clearly concerned with cultural progress. One short example from the seventeenth century is Dryden's epistle *To Sir Godfrey Kneller* recounting the history of painting ("By slow degrees the godlike art advanc'd"), and a long eighteenth-century example is Thomson's *Liberty.*

The cultural progress piece probably owes its origin to various changes of intellectual climate. As Griffith notes, the emergence and increasing popularity of the "idea of progress" would seem to be largely responsible for the congenial "fad."[46] Aubrey Williams has discussed the importance of an older but related idea, the concept of *translatio studii* or the passage of "learning" from one country to another in successive ages, which was expressed anew for the Augustans by Sir William Temple and other essayists. Williams goes on to conclude that Pope's *Dunciad* ironically turns the *translatio studii* into a *"translatio stultiae,"* ending with the complete establishment of Dulness in England.[47]

This is partly true. But it is important to notice an even more ironic aspect of the "progress" of Dulness which Pope wished to emphasize—namely, that Dulness actually *re*-establishes her authority. The intellectual "progress," in other words, is not linear but cyclical. Pope had suggested as much in his opening description of the "action" of the 1728 *Dunciad*:

> Still her old empire to confirm, she tries,
> For born a Goddess, Dulness never dies.
>
> (A, i, 15–16)

In the final version of the poem he placed even more emphasis on the cycle of duncery by changing the first line of the couplet to read, "Still her old Empire to *restore* she tries," and by noting that, with the addition of the fourth book, "this Restoration makes the Completion of the Poem."[48] Within the *Dunciad* the ideas of linear "progress" and cyclical recurrence exist side by side, and they modify one another in ways which need to be examined closely.

Commentators from Pope himself to the present have noted that Book III of the *Dunciad* is a prophetic account of the accomplishments of Dulness, "giving a glimpse, or Pisgah-sight of the future Fulness of her Glory," and Mr. Williams has discussed some of the features of the progress piece operating in the third book.[49] But Book I and, to a lesser extent, Book II contain important allusions to the Augustan conception of cultural progress which are intended to prepare the reader for the more explicit discussion of "learning" in Book III. Insofar as this heavily descriptive poem has a single action it is the "progress" which is announced in the opening proposition, namely the progress of the "Smithfield Muses to the ear of Kings." This is a progress in the twofold sense mentioned earlier, for the movement described represents both the debasement of Court taste by the City "Taste of the Rabble" and the actual Lord Mayor's procession depicted some eighty lines later.[50] The fresh memory of that pageant and its attendant celebration then provides the occasion for a recitation of modern literary history, an ironic version of the grand historical survey commonly found in progress pieces:

> Much to the mindful Queen the feast recalls
> What City Swans once sung within the walls;
> Much she revolves their arts, their ancient praise,
> And sure succession down from Heywood's days.
> She saw, with joy, the line immortal run,
> Each sire imprest and glaring in his son.
>
> (B, i, 95–100)

However ludicrous the historical context, the passage does effec-

< TEMPLE OF FAME AND "TEMPLE OF INFAMY" >

tively expand the *Dunciad's* temporal scheme, extending it back-
ward to the indeterminate "ancient praise" and forward to the
vague promise (or threat) of "sure succession." And the latter
prophetic mode is developed more fully when the goddess anoints
Cibber as the "sure" successor of Eusden:

> . . . "All hail! and hail again,
> My son! the promis'd land expects thy reign."
>   (B, i, 291–292)

Following Cibber's coronation the goddess indulges in a more
elaborate prophecy of duncical "improvement." Her declaration
of future progress is somewhat tentative since it is framed as a
rhetorical question, but the reader knows that it will be "confirmed" in the vision of Book III and the fait accompli of Book
IV:

> "O! when shall rise a Monarch all our own,
> And I, a Nursing-mother, rock the throne,
> 'Twixt Prince and People close the Curtain draw,
> Shade him from Light, and cover him from Law;
> Fatten the Courtier, starve the learned band,
> And suckle Armies, and dry-nurse the land:
> 'Till Senates nod to Lullabies divine,
> And all be sleep, as at an Ode of thine."
>   (B, i, 311–318)

In these passages, as in the long prophecy which Settle later
delivers throughout most of Book III, Pope stresses the "progression" of duncery and suggests that the power of Dulness is increasing. The implication in such a progression—and in the prophetic wish of Dulness—is that the goddess will finally attain abso-
lute monarchical authority over men's minds. In the place of a
stately advancement of learning there is an inexorable advancement of Dulness.

At the same time, however, the idea of a "sure succession" or
its geographical equivalent, a predestined *translatio*, presupposes
an unchanging continuity and perennial stability in the affairs of
Dulness. The generations and the countries may differ, but Dul-

ness is self-perpetuating, "for, born a Goddess, Dulness never dies." Thus while the *Dunciad* exploits the comic and descriptive possibilities of a linear progress of Dulness—from City to Westminster, East to West, past to present—it also deals explicitly and more seriously with the fundamentally immutable continuity of Dulness. And in this context it is not surprising that many of the poem's humorous references to "succession" or *translatio* should actually have little to do with change or progress. This paradox is present from the very beginning of the *Dunciad*, for the poet proposes to recount both the ongoing progress of "The Smithfield Muses to the ear of Kings" and the established permanence of Dulness: "Still Dunce the second reigns like Dunce the first" (B, i, 6). The word "still," of course, has here its older meaning of "perpetually" or "continually," just as it does in the line quoted previously, "Still her old Empire to restore she tries" (B, i, 17). And the permanence which these lines assign to perennial Dulness is integrated into the *Dunciad*'s invented mythology:

> In eldest time, e'er mortals writ or read,
> E'er Pallas issu'd from the Thund'rer's head,
> Dulness o'er all possess'd her ancient right,
> Daughter of Chaos and eternal Night.
>
> (B, i, 9–12)

This genealogy of Dulness is a significant feature of the "progress" Pope is about to describe, for it enlarges the poem's historical perspective and carries the reader back in "eldest" time to a primal or "native" era: "She rul'd, in native Anarchy, the mind" (B, i, 16). When Cibber, later in the same book, evokes precisely this same mythological past—" 'Secure us kindly in our native night' " (175)—his prayer to his goddess indicates that the "restoration" of Dulness is already occurring; in fact, it is always (or "still") occurring because dulness is "native" to England just as it is native to man.

Even Pope's complimentary address to Swift (probably one of the most often disregarded passages in the *Dunciad*) refers

< TEMPLE OF FAME AND "TEMPLE OF INFAMY" >

ironically to the notions of *translatio* and cultural progress. The ten-line paragraph concludes with this bit of advice on how to view Dulness:

> From thy Bœotia tho' her Pow'r retires,
> Mourn not, my SWIFT, at ought our Realm acquires,
> Here pleas'd behold her mighty wings out-spread
> To hatch a new Saturnian age of Lead.
>
> (B, i, 25–28)

Swift's "Boeotia," of course, is Ireland, and Pope explains that Boeotia "of old lay under the Raillery of the neighbouring Wits, as *Ireland* does now; tho' each of those nations produced one of the greatest Wits, and greatest Generals, of their age."[51] What these lines and Pope's note mean is that England is on the verge of becoming the modern Boeotia and that throughout history the various "learned" nations have had more in common with the Boeotians of their day than men have seen fit to acknowledge. Just as the original Boeotia was maligned by self-satisfied and self-deluded "neighbouring Wits," so Englishmen are entirely too quick to regard dulness as a non-English, foreign attribute, though in truth it is universally "native." The essential paradox of Pope's "progress" of Dulness is epitomized in these closing lines of the dedicatory paragraph, for the Boeotian "*translatio*" is not really a progress from East to West or past to present, but a comic metaphor for the abiding human propensity for mindlessness. Likewise the "new Saturnian age of Lead" is actually anything but new, as the long record of human dulness in Book III will testify.

The "progress" of the third book begins formally with a scene which recalls both the *Aeneid* and *Paradise Lost.*[52] Appointed by Dulness as Cibber's guide, Settle leads the laureate to a summit

> . . . whose cloudy point commands
> Her boundless empire over seas and lands.
>
> (B, iii, 67–68)

Then the progress outlined by Settle assumes dimensions at once geographical and temporal:

> "Far eastward cast thine eye, from whence the Sun
> And orient Science their bright course begun."
>
> (B, iii, 73–74)

The next fifty lines comprise a solemn account of the progress of Dulness from ancient China to Egypt, Greece, Rome, and finally modern England. Now, aside from the fact that Pope's survey is concerned with the depths of cultural coarseness rather than the heights of human learning, the outline of Settle's narrative is a conventional enough imitation of the progress piece which pursues its abstraction from East to West and past to present. But even here, where the progress theme is used most explicitly, Pope undercuts the very notion of temporal-geographical progress. As the conclusion of the apparent "progress" indicates, the imminent "imperial sway" of Dulness in England is anything but novel:

> This fav'rite Isle, long sever'd from her reign,
> Dove-like, she gathers to her wings again.
>
> (B, iii, 125–126)

It is just as Pope had suggested at the opening of the *Dunciad*: we are witnessing the "restoration" of the "old" empire of Dulness. In the midst of what would seem to be a direct account of linear progress Pope asserts the idea of cyclic recurrence or restoration. And he has history on his side in this counterargument since northern Europe, previously the "Great nurse of Goths . . . and of Huns" (III, 90), is simply returning to its state of "native" dulness. All nations, indeed, are seen to be continually and naturally inclining more toward ignorance than toward learning:

> "How little, mark! that portion of the ball,
> Where, faint at best, the beams of Science fall."
>
> (B, iii, 83–84)

All of this is in the spirit of the "Boeotian" paragraph of the first book, and Pope intentionally recalls that comic and paradoxical *"translatio"* in Book III. Using the metaphor of yet another kind of "progress," Settle welcomes the laureate to the

< TEMPLE OF FAME AND "TEMPLE OF INFAMY" >

"wonders of th' oblivious Lake" with a rhapsodic celebration of
the Cibberian metempsychosis:

> "Thou, yet unborn, has touch'd this sacred shore;
> The hand of Bavius drench'd thee o'er and o'er.
> But blind to former as to future fate,
> What mortal knows his pre-existent state?
> Who knows how long thy transmigrating soul
> Might from Bœotian to Bœotian roll?"
>
> (B, iii, 45–50)

The notion of metempsychosis had been brought to the aid of
serious panegyric verse in Donne's *Of the Progresse of the Soule*
(or *The Second Anniversary*), but Pope's lines come closer to
these from Dryden's ode *To Anne Killigrew*:

> But if thy preexisting soul
> Was form'd, at first, with myriads more,
> It did thro' all the mighty poets roll.
>
> (29–31)

Pope's echo of Dryden is perhaps unconscious, for he does not
call it to the reader's attention.[53] At any rate, the passage is considerably more subtle than mere mock panegyric. Whereas Settle's
speech proceeds in the form of prophecy, it is not a prophecy of
progress, either desirable or undesirable:

> "As man's Mæanders to the vital spring
> Roll all their tides, then back their circles bring;
> Or whirligigs, twirl'd round by skilful swain,
> Suck the thread in, then yield it out again:
> All nonsense thus, of old or modern date,
> Shall in thee centre, from thee circulate."
>
> (B, iii, 55–60)

Although Cibber happens to be its chosen, contemporary manifestation, dulness is of both old and modern date. There is no
"progress" finally, but only the realization of man's potential and
instinctive meanders to his native goddess.

A careful consideration of the manner and limit of Pope's use
of progress piece conventions makes clear the need to reassess the

traditional view of his intention in the *Dunciad*. Critics have assumed that Pope simply inverted the complacent force of the word "progress" by writing a "Progress of Dulness" rather than a "Progress of Learning." But his ironic mode is more complex than that. While employing many of the devices of the progress piece and, specifically, narrating a vision which extends from the ancient East to the modern West, Pope actually asserts again and again that "progress" is ultimately an irrelevant concept, a phantom notion, when the real issue is culture as the manifestation of permanent and universal human tendencies.

One cannot question the fact that Pope does "use" the progress piece as part of the *Dunciad*'s ironic context (just as, for example, he uses mock-heroic descriptions), but one may certainly question Mr. Williams's assertion that Pope uses this "minor poetic convention" to represent Dulness as an "expanding . . . force in human affairs."[54] Pope uses aspects of the genre partly for humorous incongruity, and partly because the progress piece provided a familiar means of treating an abstraction as a thing, as a fact. Pope's deepest concern is not with the "expanding" quality of Dulness but with her abiding omnipresence, symbolized by her imminent and inevitable "restoration." Turning this vision into a poem, Pope found in the conventions of the progress piece a ready way to reify his abstraction—to make Dulness, like darkness, visible. In other words, Pope exploited devices associated with the progress piece, as he had used the "temple" genre, for the peculiar descriptive license those conventions afforded him. The *Dunciad*'s indebtedness to the progress piece genre is not primarily narrative, for, as we have seen, the "progress" of dulness, discredited within the poem itself, is an illusory notion. What is not illusory, however, is the enduring abstraction of Dulness in human society. In the temple poem and in the progress piece Pope discovered what would become many of the *Dunciad*'s striking ingredients: the vaguely Platonic atmosphere of abstraction, the loose descriptive structure, the iconographic and pictorial evocation of moral identity—all of which Pope turned into a long poem "in the descriptive way . . . mixd with Vision & Moral."

< TEMPLE OF FAME AND "TEMPLE OF INFAMY" >

6.

Although the "progress" of Dulness Pope records is finally unpro-
gressive, and although his account of historical change is primarily parodic, the *Dunciad* does have some basic affinities with
the two most ambitious cultural progress pieces written during the seventeenth century. Denham's *The Progress of Learning*
(1668) and Sir Richard Fanshawe's earlier and charmingly Spenserian *Canto of the Progress of Learning* (1648) both clearly display the tendency to incorporate intellectual history into a
mythic structure.[55] To some extent, all of the more successful
progress pieces move in this direction. Implicit in the very conception of the progress piece is a conflict between the essentially
immutable, mythological realm to which the poet's personified
abstraction belongs and the temporal, historical world in which
the poem's "progress" is supposed to occur. Pope seems to have
recognized this paradox inherent in the genre, and his response
was to virtually discount the importance of linear, historical
development and to stress more forcefully the mythic and cyclic
restoration of Dulness. It is because of this latter emphasis that
Settle's more or less historical "prophecy" in Book III is ultimately no more than a tragicomic episode in a poem which begins
mythically before the beginning of history—"In eldest time, e'er
mortals writ or read"—and which ends in its own apocalypse of
"Universal Darkness." This is not to obscure the obvious fact that
the *Dunciad* is "historical" in the sense that most satire makes use
of recognizable events and people. But in the structure of the
poem history is subjugated to the logic and requisites of myth,
just as Cibber or Theobald, Bentley or Blackmore are finally significant only as the offspring of their mythical "Mighty Mother,"
Dulness. Pope mythologized cultural history more completely
than either Fanshawe or Denham, but the mythic contest between
learning and ignorance depicted in the *Dunciad* is foreshadowed
in the *Progress of Learning* as sketched by these two poets, his
most important predecessors in the task of converting the story
of man's intellectual life into descriptive verse.

The explicit mythological framework of Fanshawe's poem is drawn from Renaissance paganism, whereas Denham's "machinery" is Christian and orthodox. But the real "myth" underlying both poems comes closer to a sort of intellectual Manichaeanism, a quasi-religious vision which sees a continuing war between light or learning and darkness or ignorance. In Denham's poem, published a year after the first edition of *Paradise Lost*, this "Manichaean" struggle is clearly one between Heaven and Hell. Musing on the prophetic glimpses which God, "the Poet of the world," has granted the great human poets from time to time, Denham remarks,

> Sure God, by these Discoveries, did design
> That his clear Light through all the World should shine,
> But the Obstruction from that Discord springs
> The Prince of Darkness makes 'twixt Christian Kings.
>
> (87–90)

And just as the "Obstruction" was born out of the fall of the angels, so human ignorance is the lasting and bitter fruit of Adam's fall:

> 'Tis the most certain sign, the world's accurst,
> That the best things corrupted, are the worst;
> 'Twas the corrupted Light of knowledg, hurl'd
> Sin, Death, and Ignorance o'er all the world.
>
> (175–178)

While Denham's view of a "corrupted" world leads him to the skeptical conclusion that "sublunary Science is but guess" (198), Fanshawe begins from roughly the same premise and eventually arrives at a profession of Neoplatonic optimism. Fanshawe's original conception of ignorance might seem to be even more pessimistic than Denham's since his "progress" commences with what is actually a considerable regression in human knowledge following "ancient times." At any rate, the origin of ignorance is more vividly represented in the poem's cosmogenic, ontological myth. In the beginning—

< TEMPLE OF FAME AND "TEMPLE OF INFAMY" >

Then thus: when seeds of all things (from the wombe
    Of pregnant *Chaos* sprung) were perfected,
    Another *Chaos* (yet to be overcome)
    Out of the Reliques of the former bred,
    With ignorance this infant world orespred,
    And having drown'd Reasons deviner Ray
    In the dull lumpe of flesh, made men (the head)
    Companions of their slaves: The beasts and they
Promiscuously fed, Promiscuously lay.
                    (10–18)

The curious last line—perhaps the most eccentric alexandrine in
English poetry—sums up the notion of a primal Chaos governing
both nature and society, and Fanshawe's Chaos provides the
background for his fable of continuing strife between "Wit"
(learning or wisdom) and "Craft" (ruthless pragmatism). In such
a world the place of Learning is never secure; indeed, "Nature"
finally inclines toward the enemies of Learning. The poem ends
with true Wit eventually scorning sublunary affairs and aspiring
"unto its heav'nly country" (236). But more significant here
than Fanshawe's witty conclusion is the identification of all that
would oppose and frustrate human intelligence with a primal,
chaotic state of nature. Darkness and Chaos, in the intellectual
realm as well as the physical, are not only as old as the Creation
but older.

Seen against even this sketchy background Pope's genealogy
of Dulness as the "Daughter of Chaos and eternal Night" is considerably more than a piece of mock-heroic ridicule. It is from her
prehistoric lineage that Dulness derives her "ancient right" to
rule the mind "in native Anarchy," for in Pope's novel and secular fable she antedates the Genesis and survives the Apocalypse.
Perhaps the relation between Fanshawe's "progress" of learning
and Pope's story of Dulness is only illustrative, since there is no
evidence that Pope knew Fanshawe's poems.[56] But Fanshawe
exemplifies in the clearest terms the same poetic idea of dubious
intellectual conflict which finds expression in Denham—whose
work Pope certainly knew—as the struggle between God's "clear
Light" and the "Obstruction" and "Discord" originating from

the "Prince of Darkness."[57] When we consider the extent to which the notion of primal Chaos or Discord caught the imagination of two poets who purposed to relate the history of learning, it is not surprising that Pope, setting out to sing the permanence of Dulness, should have been able and even impelled to make the same idea the foundation of his poem's fable.

Moreover there was Milton. Students of Pope know that he assimilated Milton more sympathetically than most of the self-styled, blank-verse imitators of Milton in the eighteenth century, and much has been said concerning the particularly Miltonic quality of parts of the *Dunciad*. What needs to be emphasized here is a poetic impetus felt as strongly in the Age of Pope as in the Age of Milton—namely, a fascination with the subject of the Creation and with the states preceding its origin and following is termination. Accounts of the act of creation out of Chaos date back at least to Hesiod and to Genesis, but the second book of *Paradise Lost* is the great modern treatment of these "secrets of the hoary deep." Milton envisions the primal state as

> . . . a dark
> Illimitable Ocean without bound,
> Without dimension, where length, breadth, and height,
> And time and place are lost; where eldest Night
> And *Chaos*, Ancestors of Nature, hold
> Eternal *Anarchy*, amidst the noise
> Of endless wars, and by confusion stand.
>
> (*P.L.*, II, 892–897)

Pope imitates several specific passages from this book in the *Dunciad*, but his debt is deeply thematic as well. His derivation of Dulness from "eldest Night and Chaos" is part of a larger interest in those "Ancestors of Nature" and the "Eternal Anarchy" which represents their native condition. Milton's description of the realm of Chaos as the "Womb of nature and perhaps her Grave" enters into the world of the *Dunciad* in an especially interesting manner. Unrestrained by theological problems, Pope abandons Milton's careful, qualifying "perhaps," and the secular idea that Chaos is both the alpha and the omega becomes an

< TEMPLE OF FAME AND "TEMPLE OF INFAMY" >

imaginative fact as the shaping principle of the *Dunciad*'s narrative structure.

In *Paradise Lost*, of course, the potential power of Chaos is held in check, no less surely than the internal chaos of man, by the Creator's redemptive providence. That realm where, for the time being, "*Chance* governs all" is composed

> Of neither Sea, nor Shore, nor Air, nor Fire,
> But all these in thir pregnant causes mixt
> Confus'dly, and which thus must ever fight,
> Unless th' Almighty Maker them ordain
> His dark materials to create more Worlds.
>
> (II, 912–916)

But the *Dunciad* is not a poem about the Creator's divine ordinance: in its secular world men are left to their own resources, or rather to the insufficient resources of mankind's unchecked majority, as nature itself is allowed to run its "native" course to dissolution.

This darker aspect of the Creation—the negative and abstract quality of annihilation, nothingness, or darkness—became a poetic theme of some importance during the later seventeenth century and persisted through much of the next century. It would be convenient to say that the Age of the Enlightenment turned at last, in the 1740s, to the nocturnal emotionalism of *Night Thoughts*. But Young's immensely popular work and Pope's poetic fiction of Universal Darkness both have their roots in a small but discernible "school of night" reaching back as far as the 1670s. In a sense, Pope's oft-quoted phrase from the last line of the *Dunciad* epitomizes the attraction which annihilation held as a poetic subject, for universality and darkness seem to have gone hand in hand. For example, John Sheffield, Duke of Buckingham's *Temple of Death* (1672) shows how readily the prospect of human annihilation could serve as the focal point of a survey of mankind from China to Peru:

> Within this vale a famous temple stands,
> Old as the worlds itself, which it commands;
> Round is its figure, and four iron gates

> Divide mankind, by order of the Fates:
> Thither in crowds come to one common grave
> The young, the old, the monarch, and the slave.[58]
>
> (15–20)

These lines apparently appealed to Pope, for he seems to have echoed them in one part of the *Temple of Fame*.[59] Sheffield's poem would have also appealed to the larger audience of Augustan readers who enjoyed Rochester's loosely philosophical musings *Upon Nothing* (c. 1679), Thomas Yalden's somber *Hymn to Darkness* (1697), and Young's apocalyptic *The Last Day* (1710), as well as the so-called graveyard poems of later years.

Rochester's *Upon Nothing* is particularly interesting both because of its tough-minded sophistication and because Alexander Pope at the tender age of fourteen was moved to write a fine imitation of it, called *On Silence* (1702). Much later in the century *Upon Nothing* was still popular, and Samuel Johnson called it Rochester's "strongest effort."[60] The first three stanzas indicate how nearly allied Rochester's "Nothing" is to the Chaos described by his older contemporaries, Fanshawe and Milton:

> *NOTHING!* thou Elder Brother ev'n to Shade,
> That hadst a Being e'er the World was made,
> And (well fixt) art alone, of ending not afraid.
>
> E'er time and place were, time and place
> were not,
> When Primitive *Nothing* something strait begot,
> Than all proceeded from the great united—
> What?
>
> Something, the Gen'ral Attribute of all,
> Sever'd from thee, it's sole Original,
> Into thy boundless self must undistinguish'd fall.
>
> (1–9)

Although the "peaceful Realm" of Nothing has been temporarily conquered by the alliance of "Time" with "Matter and Form" (16–18), this nihilistic "sole Original" is both the womb and tomb of nature:

< TEMPLE OF FAME AND "TEMPLE OF INFAMY" >

But turn-Coat Time assists their Foe in vain,
And, brib'd by thee, destroys their short-lived Reign,
And to thy hungry Womb drives back thy Slaves again.
(19–21)

Pope's *On Silence* comes very close to the mood of Rochester's lines. Like Rochester, he sings the praises of a "Great Negative" that is supposed to have existed even before the Creation:

Silence! Cooeval with Eternity;
Thou wert e'er Nature's self began to be,
'Twas one vast Nothing, All, and All slept fast in thee,
Thine was the Sway, e'er Heav'n was form'd or Earth,
E'er fruitful *Thought* conceiv'd Creation's Birth,
Or Midwife *Word* gave Aid, and spoke the Infant forth.
(1–6)

Gradually the antipathy of Silence to "Thought" and "Word" intensifies and broadens, like that of Dulness in the *Dunciad*, to include all learning and intelligence:

The tongue mov'd gently first, and Speech was low,
'Till wrangling *Science* taught it Noise and Show,
And wicked *Wit* arose, thy most abusive Foe.

But Rebel Wit deserts thee oft in vain;
Lost in the Maze of Words, he turns again,
And seeks as surer State, and courts thy gentle Reign.
(10–15)

And at last Silence and Dulness are explicitly—and intimately—related to each other:

With thee in private modest *Dulness* lies,
And in thy Bosom lurks in *Thought*'s Disguise;
Thou Varnisher of *Fools*, and Cheat of all the *Wise*.
(19–21)

On Silence is not the *Dunciad* in miniature, but it does show us something of Pope's conception of Dulness in embryo. The somnolent cosmos which the young poet describes with such an easy mixture of metaphysics and satire provides the stage for a quiet, inexorable struggle between the native force of negation and the relatively short-lived order of Creation. The silent contest Pope adapted from Rochester ends finally, like the full-scale battle that would later become his own, with the dissolution of all distinctions and the preternatural "peace" of oblivious, eternal "sleep" (34–42).

No less important than the general design of the two poems are certain significant phrases which remind us how close *On Silence* is to the duncical world of Dulness. The "gentle Reign" of Silence, for example, foreshadows the yawning rule of "gentle Dulness," the "Great Tamer of all human art," who bestows "Stupefaction mild" upon all those "gently drawn" into her power. Because human intelligence is as much a potential enemy to the primeval "Sway" of Silence as it is a threat to the "Arbitrary Sway" associated with Dulness, we find it characterized in both poems as "Rebel Wit."[61]

Even more striking is the mutual opposition of Silence and Dulness to the creative power of the "Word": in *On Silence* negation is represented as antithetical to "Midwife Word"; in the *Dunciad* the realm of "CHAOS" sends forth its own "uncreating word." The abuse of the "Word" has serious intellectual (and spiritual) implications, and so it is small wonder that Silence is as much supported by that intelligence which ends "Lost in the Maze of Words" as Dulness is strengthened by those votaries who would keep the human spirit "in the pale of Words till death."[62]—Small wonder, that is, but for the fact that the poet who lisped these imitative numbers tentatively at the beginning of his career should return some forty years later, in the final book of his final poem, to call forth their implicit grandeur and sing them with new and terrible sureness.

7.

When Pope translated the last book of the *Iliad* he described the grieving Achilles as a man deprived of even the comfort of "all-composing Sleep" (XXIV, 8). The incidental epithet apparently stayed in Pope's mind, and in the inverted world of the

< TEMPLE OF FAME AND "TEMPLE OF INFAMY" >

Dunciad, where sleep always comes too easily, the "all-composing Hour" (IV, 627) marks the conquest of sleep and dissolution over the light of intelligence and the order of creation. Pope's use of the "Homeric" epithet at this point is more than mock heroic, for the function of Dulness is to "blot out" (IV, 14) those distinctions upon which order and existence depend, to "compose" the once ordered universe of art and nature into uncreating and universal darkness.

Universal darkness, as I mentioned, was not an uncommon subject in seventeenth- and eighteenth-century poetry, and one final example of its treatment may help render this darkness visible. Thomas Yalden's *Hymn to Darkness* (1710) is a minor poem by a minor poet, but Yalden's evocative discussion of universal darkness and "universal ruin" seems to have influenced Pope's final conception of Dulness and uncreation as strongly as did Rochester's *Upon Nothing* and Pope's own *On Silence*.

Describing Darkness as our ultimate "parent," "great original," and "universal womb," Yalden proceeds to explain the present role Darkness plays in the universe:

> The silent globe is struck with awful fear,
>   When thy majestic shades appear:
>   Thou dost *compose* the air and sea,
> And Earth a *sabbath* keeps, sacred to Rest and Thee.
>
>   (17–20, my italics)

In Yalden's poem, as in the *Dunciad*, sleep is associated with the heavier sleep of potential extinction, and his phrases suggest the "one heavy sabbath" somnolescently embracing "all the Western World" in Book III as well as the apocalyptic "all-composing Hour" of Book IV. In both poems the tendency toward dissolution is seen to spring from the same fatality, since Darkness resembles Dulness most closely in its lack of regard for distinctions:

> Thou dost thy smiles impartially bestow,
>   And know'st no difference here below:
>   All things appear the same by thee,
> Though Light distinctions makes, thou giv'st equality.
>
>   (37–40)

But light and enlightened distinctions are only temporary forces. The energy which animates the creation is destined to give way before the world's anterior and annihilating "Monarch":

> Yet fading Light its empire must resign,
> And Nature's power submit to thine:
> An universal ruin shall erect thy throne,
> And Fate confirm thy kingdom evermore thy own.

(69–72)

Although one cannot point to a direct historical relation between Yalden's Darkness and Pope's Dulness, the similarities do suggest kinship. The similarities also suggest the extent to which Pope wished to make Dulness a credible abstraction and the real subject of his poem. We see, moreover, that an Augustan reader might easily have warmed to such a universal and negative abstraction.

It has often been pointed out that numerous satiric writers had personified Dulness in verse and prose by the time Pope wrote the *Dunciad*. But even in the best of these satires, *MacFlecknoe*, the personification of Dulness or "Nonsense" is a comic vehicle carrying personal ridicule quickly and lightly. There is much personal ridicule in the *Dunciad*, too; but the personification of Dulness ultimately *is* the poem. By conflating the present with "eldest" and future time, by transmuting historical and fictional characters into a preternatural allegorical scene, and by drawing both fable and phrase from various poems—including his own—which describe cosmic abstractions, Pope made his "Temple of Infamy" or "Poem of Dulness" a grand metaphor for the "all-composing" disintegration "native" to unredeemed art, society, and nature. It is Scriblerus who has the last word. Although the personalities of the dunces animate parts of the poem, when we consider the *Dunciad* as a whole, Cibber, Theobald, Blackmore, Bentley, and the rest are, as Pope's annotator had insisted in a lighter mood, "all phantoms."

What remains after the phantoms vanish is Pope's massive and moving achievement. To try to prove that the *Dunciad* is a great

< TEMPLE OF FAME AND "TEMPLE OF INFAMY" >

poem seems to me as circular as it is presumptuous, for this study began with that premise. But I think readers of Pope may find the *Dunciad* moving for reasons not solely aesthetic. The poem is, after all else has been said, quite personal in what it reveals about Pope as a poet. I am not speaking now of all the *Dunciad*'s "personal" satire, retaliation, or provocation. More personal by far is the amalgamation, in Pope's last and longest poem, of many of the poetic concerns that were present from the very beginning of his career. At times, particularly in the works of the 1730s, Pope is one of the most worldly of poets. During the first half of his life as a poet, however, he also felt a strong attraction for a shadowy, otherworldly kind of poetry. It is this sort of poem that he first attempted, as a boy, in *On Silence*, that he returned to, as a young man, in the more ambitious *Temple of Fame*, and that he recommended still later, from his translator's desk, to Judith Cowper as a "Vision." Perhaps Pope's great Horatian poems and the *Essay on Man* are denials of the poet's long-felt inclination for otherworldly vision; they are, at any rate, poems of contemporary social existence. But in the *Dunciad* Pope was free to synthesize both worlds, bringing together topics both temporal and timeless, concrete and abstract, highly factual and profoundly mythic. As early as *On Silence* we glimpse Pope's secular vision of human time as a brief moment of order destined to revert to native darkness and chaos. In the *Temple of Fame* we see him treading the area between cultural history and static abstraction. The "Temple of Infamy," which he finished building only a year before his death, combines the cosmic truth of these "visions" with the worldly truth of Pope's energetic involvement in the present. The *Dunciad* is the product of a great life's work.

NOTES AND LIST OF WORKS CITED

Notes

INTRODUCTION

1. *The Correspondence of Alexander Pope,* ed. George Sherburn (Oxford, 1956), III, 36. The letter is dated 30 May 1729.

2. Austin Warren, *Alexander Pope as Critic and Humanist* (Princeton, 1929). *The Twickenham Edition of the Poems of Alexander Pope,* ed. John Butt et al., 10 vols. (London, 1939–1967). Aubrey L. Williams, *Pope's "Dunciad": A Study of Its Meaning* (London and Baton Rouge, 1955).

3. Williams, p. 5.

CHAPTER I: "How Farce and Epic Get a Jumbled Race": Generic Confusion

1. *The Critical Works of John Dennis,* ed. Edward Niles Hooker (Baltimore, 1939–1943), II, 361.

2. *Twickenham Edition,* V, xli–xlii. Ian Jack, *Augustan Satire: Intention and Idiom in English Poetry, 1660–1750* (Oxford, 1952), pp. 127–128, 131. Williams, pp. 9–41. See "Martinus Scriblerus, of the Poem," *Twickenham Edition,* V, 51; Williams, p. 8; Reuben Brower, *Alexander Pope: The Poetry of Allusion* (Oxford, 1959), pp. 344–345.

3. *Twickenham Edition,* V, xliv.

4. This point has been made by various critics. In particular see Williams, p. 59, and Alvin B. Kernan, "The *Dunciad* and the Plot of Satire," *SEL,* II (1962), 255–266.

5. Jack, pp. 130–131.

6. All quotations are from the *Dunciad,* ed. James Sutherland, 3rd ed. (London and New Haven, 1963). In his edition (Volume V of the *Twickenham Edition*) Mr. Sutherland has printed the 1729 *Dunciad Variorum* as "Dunciad (A)" and the 1743 text as "Dunciad (B)." Following this system, I have used "A" or "B" as prefixes to indicate from which text I am quoting.

Poetry of Pope's *Dunciad*

7. Max Bluestone has discussed Pope's use later in the first book (B, i, 118–126) of what he calls the "finely turned grotesquerie of gestation." See "The Suppressed Metaphor in Pope," *Essays in Criticism*, VIII (1958), 347–354.

8. This couplet is from a poem entitled "The Devil, a Wife, and a Poet. A Satyr. Occasion'd by a late Paraphrase on the Book of Job," which was printed in *The Grove; or, A Collection of Original Poems, Translations, Etc.* (London, 1721), pp. 39–52. The relevant lines in the 1729 *Dunciad* are 111–116, which begin "Studious he sate, with all his *books* around" (my italics). This is literary denigration similar to the reference to Blackmore's "Reams of Verse" in the anonymous satire referred to. The revised passage (B, i, 121–126) combines literary and physical denigration.

9. *An Apology for the Life of Mr. Colley Cibber, Comedian* (London, 1740).

10. See *Twickenham Edition*, V, 286–287.

11. The couplet alluded to is Rochester's translation of Seneca's *"post mortem nihil est"*: "And to that Mass of Matter shall be swept/ Where things destroy'd, with things unborn are kept." See *Poems by John Wilmot, Earl of Rochester*, ed. Vivian de Sola Pinto, 2nd ed. (Cambridge, Mass., 1964), p. 49.

12. Pope has made the connection between the Cave and the Dome rather unclear. In a note to the line "She bids him wait her to her sacred Dome" (for which see *Twickenham Edition*, V, 89–90), Pope equates the two. But Cibber (or Theobald) is first seen *in* the Cave and then conducted *to* the Dome within the narrative of the poem itself. For this reason I regard them as separate places and discuss them as such.

13. See especially VI, 921–973, in Dryden's translation.

14. A convenient summary of the extensive scholarship concerning possible sources of Spenser's Garden is to be found in *The Works of Edmund Spenser. A Variorum Edition*, ed. Edwin Greenlaw, Charles G. Osgood, and Frederick M. Padelford (Baltimore, 1934), III, 340–352.

15. Jack, p. 129; Brower, p. 332.

16. *Correspondence*, II, 189. The letter is undated, but Sherburn assigns it to August of 1723.

17. As Pope and others have noted, the passage is in part a burlesque imitation of Virgil's description of *"infelix"* Nisus (*Aeneid*, V, 329–333). Perhaps more to the point is the plight of Pope's own "unhappy" Ajax who slips on "slimy Dung" (Pope's *Iliad*, XXIII, 905–914).

18. The passage imitates *Paradise Lost*, II, 947–950.

19. Williams, pp. 56–57.

20. See *Twickenham Edition*, V, pp. 106–107. (Pope's phrase is a slight misquotation of Addison's comment on Virgil's style in the Georgics.)

21. Pope prided himself on such effects throughout his life. A few weeks before his death he remarked to Spence: "I have followed that (the significance of the numbers and the adapting them to the sense) much more even than Dryden, and much oftener than anyone minds it: particularly in the translations of Homer, where 'twas most necessary to do so, and in the *Dunciad* often, and indeed in all my poems" (Joseph Spence, *Observations, Anecdotes, and Characters of Books and Men*, ed. James Osborne [Oxford, 1966], I, 173–174). If "The Sound must seem an Eccho to the Sense" (*Essay on Criticism*, 365), then senselessness might be justly rendered by meaningless dissonance.

22. See *Twickenham Edition*, V, 176. Pope's use of the stage as microcosm and macrocosm is discussed extensively and perceptively in Aubrey Williams's chapter "A Theatre for Worldlings," pp. 87–103.

< NOTES >

23. H. H. Erskine-Hill discusses several passages from the *Dunciad* in which matter and manner are apparently at odds and concludes (rightly, I think) that Pope often found the "imagined world of folly" to be "fascinating" as well as "repulsive." See "The 'New World' of Pope's *Dunciad,*" *Renaissance and Modern Studies,* VI (1962), 58. In his fine reading of the *Dunciad* (*This Dark Estate* [Berkeley and Los Angeles, 1963], pp. 112–130), Thomas R. Edwards, Jr., comments on the envisioned reversal of natural order.

24. Pope annotates this passage: "It is reported of *Aeschylus,* that when his Tragedy of the *Furies* was acted, the audience were so terrify'd that the children fell into fits, and the big-bellied women miscarried" (*Twickenham Edition,* V, p. 185). The text of the poem itself suggests literary abortions as well as literary terrors.

25. *Paradise Lost,* XII, 587 and IV, 20.

26. Williams suggests (p. 151) that the phrase "dove-like" implies that "Dulness is . . . (in one of her aspects) God the un-Holy Spirit."

27. Kernan characterizes the "plot" of the *Dunciad* as an "expansion-contraction pattern" (*Studies in English Literature,* II [1962], p. 266). This statement is, I think, an exaggeration of Kernan's more accurate statement that the "spread of dulness is a contraction of life."

28. Williams, p. 141.

29. Brower, pp. 342–343.

30. Ibid., p. 342. F. R. Leavis, *The Common Pursuit* (London, 1952), p. 91; Williams, pp. 6, 88.

31. J. F. Senault, *The Use of the Passions,* trans. Henry, Earl of Monmouth (London, 1649). Maynard Mack notes Pope's apparent indebtedness to Senault (in expression as well as in theory) in the *Essay on Man.* See especially *Twickenham Edition,* III, i, 47, 68, 69, 77.

The passage is a total reversal of Pope's optimistic conclusion to *Windsor Forest* ("In Brazen Bonds shall barb'rous *Discord* dwell . . .").

32. Erwin Panofsky, *Studies in Iconology* (Oxford, 1939; Harper Torchbook reprint, 1962), p. 195. I have necessarily simplified a very detailed discussion: Panofsky indicates that chained figures sometimes represent the subjection *of* or the enslavement *by* the passions and emotions. Particularly relevant is his discussion (pp. 194–199) of the Renaissance "Victory" group, in which fettered captives apparently allegorize the triumph of good over evil. In Pope's description the triumph is inverted.

33. Jack, pp. 125–126.

34. *The Garden and the City: Retirement and Politics in the Later Poetry of Pope, 1731–1743* (Toronto, 1969), p. 180.

35. Jack, p. 118.

36. Brower, p. 361.

CHAPTER II: "The Miltons of a Curl":
Epic Inversion

1. Dryden spoke of "the genius of the age" in connection with Elizabethan drama. See, for example, "Heads of an Answer to Rymer" (1677) in *Of Dramatic Poesy and Other Critical Essays,* ed. George Watson (London, 1962), I, 214. The development of the historical study of literature is traced in René Wellek's standard account, *The Rise of English Literary History* (Chapel Hill, 1941), pp. 14–26 of which are particularly relevant to my discussion.

2. *Twickenham Edition,* VII, 14. "The Preface of the Editor" to *The*

Works of Shakespeare (1725), in *Eighteenth-Century Critical Essays,* ed. Scott Elledge (Ithaca, 1961), I, 281.

3. *Spectator,* No. 60, 9 May 1711.

4. *Twickenham Edition,* V, 131.

5. For discussions of Blackmore's literary relations see Richard C. Boys, *Sir Richard Blackmore and the Wits* (Ann Arbor, 1949), and Albert Rosenberg, *Sir Richard Blackmore: A Poet and Physician of the Augustan Age* (Lincoln, Neb., 1953). In an ingenious but wrongheaded article, John C. Hodges argues that certain features of the *Dunciad* derive from Blackmore's own satiric poem, *Kit-Cats* (1708); the only apparent similarity, however, is that both Blackmore and Pope (like various other writers) made Dulness a divinity and that both had read Garth's *Dispensary* ("Pope's Debt to One of His Dunces," *Modern Language Notes,* LI [1936], 154–158).

6. *Twickenham Edition,* V, 130.

7. Ibid., xli.

8. See H. T. Swedenberg, Jr., *The Theory of the Epic in England, 1650–1800* (Berkeley, 1944), pp. 166–193.

9. *Essays upon Several Subjects* (London, 1716), pp. 88–89, 49–50.

10. *The Critical Works of John Dennis,* II, 113–114.

11. Preface to *Prince Arthur,* quoted in Swedenberg, p. 312; *Essays,* pp. 176–177.

12. *Twickenham Edition,* V, 269.

13. *Essays,* p. 89.

14. Ibid., p. 79. Swedenberg concludes that Augustan authorities "were almost unanimously agreed that the epic action should have a fortunate conclusion" (p. 169).

15. Sutherland, *Twickenham Edition,* V, xv; cf. W. L. MacDonald's description of the *Peri Bathous* as the "scherzo movement" in *Pope and His Critics* (London, 1951), p. 167.

16. *Peri Bathous: Or, Martinus Scriblerus His Treatise of the Art of Sinking in Poetry* (London, 1727), p. 6. (I have used the facsimile of this edition, ed. Edna L. Steeves, New York, 1952.)

17. The traditional assumption that Pope was parodying Le Bossu in his "Receipt" was first challenged by Austin Warren (pp. 168–169), and Loyd Douglas has since demonstrated convincingly that Blackmore was the prime target of Pope's satire ("'A Severe Animadversion on Bossu,'" *PMLA,* LXII [1947], 690–706).

18. Geoffrey Tillotson, *On the Poetry of Pope,* 2nd ed. (Oxford, 1950), p. 55.

19. A Pope-Warburton note to IV, 7, associates the "Force inertly strong" of Dulness with the "Vis inertiae of Matter."

20. "On Reading Pope," *College English,* VII (1946), 273.

21. "Remarks on *Prince Arthur*" (1696) in *The Critical Works of John Dennis,* I, 56.

22. *Essays,* p. 74.

CHAPTER III: The *Temple of Fame* and the
"Temple of Infamy"

1. See *Twickenham Edition,* V, 59–60 and 201–206, for Pope's notes to the title, first line, and Appendix I ("The Publisher to the Reader"); Sutherland

< NOTES >

also discusses the circumstances preceding the *Dunciad*'s publication in his introduction, p. xvii.

2. A letter to this effect appeared in the *Daily Journal* for 11 May 1728, a week before the *Dunciad* appeared. Later Pope attributed this sarcastic letter to John Dennis. Probably as a blind, the first duodecimo edition of the *Dunciad* contained an advertisement for a forthcoming *Progress of Dulness* by "an eminent hand." See *Twickenham Edition,* V, xvii–xxiv.

3. *Correspondence,* II, 468, 480.

4. See Reginald Harvey Griffith, "The Progress Pieces of the Eighteenth Century," *Texas Review,* V (1920), 218–233. Griffith's study is still the most nearly comprehensive treatment of this significant genre. Although he refers to Lansdowne's *Progress of Beauty* (1701) as the form's "earliest true exemplar," recognizable progress pieces date back at least to the mid-seventeenth century. See also Mattie Swayne, "The Progress Piece in the Seventeenth Century," *University of Texas Studies in English* (1936), pp. 84–92, and Alan D. McKillop, "Griffith's Pioneer Study of the Progress Piece," *The Great Torch Race,* ed. Mary Tom Osborne (Austin, 1961), pp. 45–57.

5. Geoffrey Tillotson, ed., *Twickenham Edition,* II, 242–244.

6. The original couplet (A, ii, 293–294) was first changed in the 1735 folio of Pope's *Works; Twickenham Edition,* V, 312.

7. *Twickenham Edition,* V, 205.

8. Pope's use of his source is discussed at length in Tillotson's introduction and by A. C. Cawley, "Chaucer, Pope, and Fame," *Review of English Literature,* III (1962), 9–19; *Twickenham Edition,* II, 250, 222.

9. Ll. 240–244. All quotations from the *Hous of Fame* are from *The Works of Geoffrey Chaucer,* ed. Fred N. Robinson (Cambridge, Mass., 1957).

10. For a discussion of the close relation between Venus and Fame in Chaucer's poem see J. A. W. Bennett, *Chaucer's "Book of Fame"* (Oxford, 1968), pp. 1–51.

11. *Twickenham Edition,* II, 270.

12. "This notion of fame . . . looks back to the Renaissance poets and forward to the Romantic poets: it would have won the approval of Spenser no less than Byron. But it is alien to Chaucer's way of thinking and is far removed from the sceptical view of fame expressed by him in his poem on this subject" (Cawley, p. 19).

13. The modern and exclusive sense of "intellectual" (i.e., "possessing a high degree of understanding; given to pursuits that exercise the intellect") is first exemplified in the *OED* by a couplet from Byron's *Don Juan* (I, xxii). Pope's couplet, on the other hand, is the *latest* citation in the same source for the now virtually obsolete meaning, "non-material, spiritual; apprehended by the intellect alone (as distinguished from what is perceived by the senses), ideal." I should think it possible that the word "intellectual" had "learned" connotations long before the Romantic period.

14. *Twickenham Edition,* II, 270.

15. See ll. 1465–1480.

16. *Paradise Lost,* II, 1–5, cited in Pope's note (*Twickenham Edition,* V, 96). Williams points out that a large share of the passages from *Paradise Lost* which Pope ironically imitates are drawn from descriptions of Satan or the other fallen angels (pp. 131–141).

17. "Camillo Querno," Pope informs the reader, "was introduced as a Buffoon" to Pope Leo X "and promoted to the honour of the Laurel; a jest

125

which the Court of *Rome* and the Pope himself entered into" (*Twickenham Edition*, V, 97).

18. Pope's note to A, ii, 60 (ibid., 105) quotes *Paradise Lost,* II, 947–950.

19. "Mother Osborne" is not Thomas Osborne, the bookseller who made his way into literary history by provoking Samuel Johnson to blows, but rather James Pitt, who wrote under the pseudonym Francis Osborne (*Twickenham Edition,* V, 311, 451).

20. These lines (A, ii, 271–272) originally referred to John Dennis. While the second line alludes, as Pope notes, to Ovid's description of Milo (*Twickenham Edition,* V, 135), the first line is a distinct echo of Milton's description of Adam and Eve, who "In naked Majesty seem'd Lords of all" (IV, 290). It has been suggested to me by Mr. David Morris of the University of Virginia that the 1728 couplet thus "parodies Dennis' plan to return poetry to its original innocence and perhaps his earlier position as 'The Critic'—or, Lord, of all." The couplet was revised after Dennis had died.

21. The most extensive study of this aspect of Pope's poetry is Benjamin Boyce's *The Character-Sketches in Pope's Poems* (Durham, 1962).

22. The lines on "Atticus" finally came to rest in the *Epistle to Dr. Arbuthnot* (193–214); the second passage is from the *Epistle to a Lady* (87–100).

23. *Twickenham Edition,* V, xli. For an opposing view see R. H. Griffith's review of Sutherland's edition in *Philological Quarterly,* XXIV (1945), 155.

24. *Twickenham Edition,* II, 251–252.

25. Boyce, p. 24.

26. The terms "fable" and "action" were used by Augustan critics with only partial agreement on their meanings. The problem is discussed by Swedenberg in *The Theory of the Epic in England,* pp. 166–169.

27. Much of Pope's knowledge of the Northern peoples derived from Temple's essay "Of Heroic Virtue," and he assumed also Temple's mixed regard for the "principle of religion or superstition" which led Northern warriors to seek death in battle as "the entrance into another life." "Their bodies indeed were hard and strong . . . their courage was undaunted, their business was war, their pleasures were dangers, their very sports were martial; their disputes and processes were divided by arms; they feared nothing but too long life, decays of age, and a natural or slothful death—any violent or bloody they desired and pursued; and all this from their opinion of one being succeeded by miseries, the other by felicities, of a future and a longer life." See *Five Miscellaneous Essays by Sir William Temple,* ed. Samuel Holt Monk (Ann Arbor, 1963), pp. xxxvi, 141–146. The complex and changing English attitude toward things "Gothic" is the subject of Samuel Kliger's interesting study, *The Goths in England* (Cambridge, Mass., 1952).

28. *Correspondence,* II, 202–203. The letter is dated 26 September 1723.

29. Pope's one other "Chaucerian" poem *is* only an exercise: "A Tale of Chaucer. Lately found in an old Manuscript" (*Twickenham Edition,* VI, 41–42), an amusing but superficial imitation.

30. Exactly when Pope began to write the *Dunciad* is unknown. Definite allusions to the poem do not appear before the beginning of 1728, but it is likely that parts were written earlier. (See *Twickenham Edition,* V, ix–xvii.) On 14 September 1725 Pope wrote Swift: "Your travels [i.e., *Gulliver's Travels*] I hear much of; my own, I promise you, shall never more be in a strange land, but a diligent, I hope useful, investigation of my own territories. I mean no more translations, but something domestic, fit for my own country, and for my own time" (*Correspondence,* II, 321–322). Warburton later cited

< NOTES >

this letter as a reference to Pope's plan for the *Essay on Man,* but he appears to have had no authority for doing so other than his characteristic self-assurance. It is more likely that Pope's intention to write something fit for his "own country" and "own time" refers to the *Dunciad.* A similiar allusion a month later almost certainly points to a daring satire rather than a vindication of the ways of God to man: "I won't tell you [Swift] what designes I have in my head . . . till I see you here, face to face. Then you shall have no reason to complain of me, for want of a Generous disdain of this World, or of the loss of my ears, in yours and Their service" (*Correspondence,* II, 333).

31. *The Critical Works of John Dennis,* II, 362.

32. Following *The Shepherd's Week,* Swift suggested to Gay that he write a "Newgate pastoral," and the eventual result was the *Beggar's Opera.* Swift made the suggestion indirectly in a letter to Pope dated 30 August 1716 (*Correspondence of Jonathan Swift,* ed. Harold Williams [Oxford, 1963], II, 215).

33. This particular epithet occurs twice, at B, ii, 417, and B, iii, 231.

34. Garth's personified "Horoscope" in the *Dispensary* is referred to as the "Magus" (see particularly cantos II and III). Martin C. Battestin argues that Fielding's oblique characterization of Walpole as a "magus" in the mock-heroic *Vernoniad* (1741) is the source for this section of *Dunciad* IV. See "Pope's 'Magus' in Fielding's *Vernoniad*: The Satire of Walpole," *Philological Quarterly,* XLVI (1967), 137–141.

35. In addition to works cited elsewhere, some of the more interesting studies of the fourth book are John W. Crowther, Jr., "Pope's Defense of Theology, Philosophy and the Arts in *Dunciad* IV," in *Essays and Studies in Language and Literature,* ed. Herbert H. Petit (Pittsburgh, 1964), pp. 133–137; Arthur Friedman, "Pope and Deism (The *Dunciad,* IV, 459–492)," in *Pope and His Contemporaries,* ed. James Clifford and Louis Landa (Oxford, 1949), pp. 89–95; William J. Howard, "The Mystery of the Cibberian *Dunciad,*" *Studies in English Literature,* VIII (1968), 463–474.

36. "The *Dunciad,* Book IV," *University of Texas Studies in English,* (1944), pp. 174–190; "Literary Backgrounds to Book Four of the *Dunciad,*" *PMLA,* LXVIII (1953), 806–813. For an account of the "session" satire (both verse and prose) from Boccalini's "De' Ragguagli Di Parnasso" (Venice, 1612) to Sheffield's "Election of a Poet Laureat in 1719" (London, 1723) see Hugh Macdonald's introduction to his edition of *A Journal from Parnassus* (London, 1937).

37. The adjective is Sherburn's (p. 179).

38. A. C. Cawley, "Chaucer, Pope, and Fame," *Review of English Literature,* III (1962), 18. Cawley writes: "Pope, no less than Chaucer, is convinced that the desire for fame is a ruling passion in the majority of men. In the *Dunciad,* IV, 73, he refers to 'The young, the old, who feel her inward sway.' " Both the context and Pope's note to IV, 71, however, leave no doubt concerning the irony of the passage.

39. Cawley (pp. 18–19) notes that Chaucer depicts a second group of hermits, asking, like the first, to go unnoticed. *Their* request is quickly granted. Pope characterizes Fame as slightly less capricious by substituting the band of soldiers for the second group of hermits.

40. Not only are Annius and Mummius alike to the point of being indistinguishable, but they are also, Pope suggests, effeminate "lovers": upon reconciliation, they leave happily "hand in Hand." An interesting reading of this section is Jessie Rhodes Chambers's article, "The Episode of Annius and

Mummius: *Dunciad* IV, 347–396," *Philological Quarterly,* XLIII (1964), 185–192.

41. Gilbert Highet, "The *Dunciad*," *Modern Language Review,* XXXVI (1941), 320–343. Highet's article, no longer taken seriously, begins with the premise that the *Dunciad* is "quite obviously a failure," capable of being admired only by those who have "either an uncritical love for Pope's reputation or an unenviable pleasure in sheer spite" (p. 320).

42. See, for example, Brower, pp. 332–335, Tillotson, p. 55, and Jack, p. 129.

43. "But General Satire in Times of General Vice has no force, & is no Punishment: People have ceas'd to be ashamed of it when so many are joind with them; and tis only by hunting One or two from the Herd that any Examples can be made" (Pope to Arbuthnot, 2 August 1734, *Correspondence,* III, 423).

44. *Twickenham Edition,* V, xvii, xxi–xxii.

45. Griffith, p. 218.

46. Ibid., pp. 224–225. The classic study of the idea of progress is J. B. Bury's *The Idea of Progress: A Collection of Readings* (Berkeley and Los Angeles, 1949).

47. Williams, pp. 46–47.

48. For B, i, 17, and Pope's note see *Twickenham Edition,* V, 270; the italics in the quotation are mine.

49. Williams, pp. 42–48. Although my estimate of the relation between the progress piece and the *Dunciad* differs considerably from that of Williams's, I am indebted to his discussion.

50. Pope's note makes his meaning explicit: "*Smithfield* is the place where Bartholomew Fair was kept, whose Shews, Machines, and Dramatic Entertainments, formerly agreeable only to the taste of the Rabble, were . . . brought . . . to be the reigning Pleasures of the Court and Town" (*Twickenham Edition,* V, 60).

51. Ibid., 62.

52. Pope's underworld and "prophecy" are comic imitations of the Sixth Book of the *Aeneid* (as several of his notes point out) and the last two books of *Paradise Lost* (which, of course, are also indebted to Virgil). See Williams's chapter "The Anti-Christ of Wit" (pp. 131–158) for a thorough and perceptive discussion of Pope's Miltonic imitation.

53. Pope does not note many of his echoes of various poets, ancient and modern, but he does point out most of the instances where solemn language (such as Miltonic description) is transferred to a ludicrous subject (such as Curll). Dryden is cited several times in Pope's notes, but neither he nor Mr. Sutherland records this borrowing from the ode *To Anne Killigrew*.

54. See Williams, pp. 46–48.

55. All references to Denham's poem are to the text of Theodore Howard Banks, Jr., ed., *The Poetical Works of Sir John Denham* (New Haven, 1928). There is no complete modern edition of Fanshawe's poetry, but the *Canto* is available in N. W. Bawcutt's collection, *Shorter Poems and Translations of Sir Richard Fanshawe* (Liverpool, 1964).

56. Pope does not mention Fanshawe in his correspondence, and he is not included in the manuscript list of poets whom Pope "classed . . . according to their several schools and successions." (These notes for a "discourse on the rise and progress of English poetry" were included in Owen Ruffhead's *Life of Alexander Pope, Esq.* [London, 1769], p. 425.) Omission from this list, of course, means merely that Pope did not consider Fanshawe a "major" figure in literary history, and that verdict is not likely to be reversed.

< NOTES >

57. IV, 590 ("Or draw to silk Arachne's subtile line") is almost certainly a reference to 1, 195, of *The Progress of Learning*.

58. Sheffield's poem is a translation of Phillipe Habert's *Le Temple de la Mort*, which had been published in Paris in 1646. The English poem is reprinted in Johnson's *Works of the English Poets* (London, 1779-1781), XXXII, 11-20.

59. Cf. *Temple of Fame*, 65-69:

> Four Faces had the Dome, and ev'ry Face
> Of various Structure, but of equal Grace:
> Four brazen Gates, on Columns lifted high,
> Salute the diff'rent Quarters of the Sky.

60. *The Lives of the Poets*, ed. G. Birkbeck Hill (Oxford, 1905), I, 224. The date of *On Silence* is approximate: it was first published in 1712 but probably written a decade earlier. See *Twickenham Edition*, VI, 19.

61. Dulness is characterized as "gentle" at B, ii, 34, and as the "Great Tamer of all human art" at B, i, 163. In addition to "Stupefaction mild" (IV, 530), Dulness also exudes a "Vapour mild" (IV, 615); in addition to "Rebel Wit" (IV, 158), the goddess also quells "rebellious Logic" (IV, 23) and all those "weak rebels" (IV, 86) who are "gently drawn" (IV, 83) into her Vortex.

62. To "keep them in the pale of Words till death" is Dr. Busby's pedagogical program (IV, 160).

List of Works Cited

Ault, Norman. "Pope and 'England's Arch-poet,'" *Review of English Studies,* XIX (1943), 376–385.

Battestin, Martin C. "Pope's 'Magus' in Fielding's *Vernoniad*: The Satire of Walpole," *Philological Quarterly,* XLVI (1967), 137–141.

Bennett, J. A. W. *Chaucer's "Book of Fame."* Oxford, 1968.

Blackmore, Sir Richard. *Essays upon Several Subjects.* 2 vols. London, 1716.

Bluestone, Max. "The Suppressed Metaphor in Pope," *Essays in Criticism,* VIII (1958), 347–354.

Boyce, Benjamin. *The Character-Sketches in Pope's Poems.* Durham, 1962.

Boys, Richard C. *Sir Richard Blackmore and the Wits.* University of Michigan Contributions in Philology, No. 13, Ann Arbor, 1949.

Brower, Reuben. *Alexander Pope: The Poetry of Allusion.* Oxford, 1959.

Bury, J. B. *The Idea of Progress: An Inquiry into Its Origin and Growth.* New York, 1932.

Cawley, A. C. "Chaucer, Pope, and Fame," *Review of English Literature,* III (1962), 9–19.

Chambers, Jessie Rhodes. "The Episode of Annius and Mummius: *Dunciad* IV, 347–96," *Philological Quarterly,* XLIII (1964), 185–192.

Cibber, Colley. *An Apology for the Life of Mr. Colley Cibber, Comedian.* London, 1740.

Clifford, James L., and Louis A. Landa, eds. *Pope and His Contemporaries: Essays Presented to George Sherburn.* Oxford, 1949.

Crowther, John W., Jr. "Pope's Defense of Theology, Philosophy and the Arts in *Dunciad* IV," in *Essays and Studies in Language and Literature,* ed. Herbert H. Petit. Pittsburgh, 1964.

Denham, Sir John. *The Poetical Works of Sir John Denham,* ed. Theodore Howard Banks, Jr. New Haven, 1928.

Dennis, John. *The Critical Works of John Dennis,* ed. Edward Niles Hooker. 2 vols. Baltimore, 1939–1943.

< WORKS CITED >

Douglas, Loyd. " 'A Severe Animadversion on Bossu,' " *PMLA*, LXII (1947), 690–706.

Dryden, John. *Of Dramatic Poesy and Other Critical Essays*, ed. George Watson. 2 vols. London, 1962.

Edwards, Thomas R., Jr. *This Dark Estate: A Reading of Pope*. Berkeley and Los Angeles, 1963.

Elledge, Scott. *Eighteenth Century Critical Essays*, 2 vols. Ithaca, 1961.

Erskine-Hill, H. H. "The 'New World' of Pope's *Dunciad*," *Renaissance and Modern Studies*, VI (1962), 49–67.

Fanshawe, Sir Richard. *Shorter Poems and Translations*, ed. N. W. Bawcutt. Liverpool, 1964.

Garth, Sir Samuel. *Dispensary*, ed. Wilhelm Josef Leicht. Heidelberg, 1905.

Griffith, Reginald Harvey. "The Progress Pieces of the Eighteenth Century," *Texas Review*, V (1920), 218–233.

_____. Review of the Twickenham *Dunciad*, *Philological Quarterly*, XXIV (1945), 152–157.

Grove; or, A Collection of Original Poems, Translations, Etc., The. London, 1721.

Highet, Gilbert. "The *Dunciad*," *Modern Language Review*, XXXVI (1941), 320–343.

Hodges, John C. "Pope's Debt to One of His Dunces," *Modern Language Notes*, LI (1936), 154–158.

Howard, William J. "The Mystery of the Cibberian *Dunciad*," *Studies in English Literature*, VIII (1968), 463–474.

Jack, Ian. *Augustan Satire: Intention and Idiom in English Poetry, 1660–1750*. Oxford, 1952.

Johnson, Samuel. *Lives of the English Poets*, ed. G. Birkbeck Hill. 3 vols. Oxford, 1905.

Kernan, Alvin B. "The *Dunciad* and the Plot of Satire," *Studies in English Literature*, II (1962), 255–266.

Kliger, Samuel. *The Goths in England: A Study in Seventeenth and Eighteenth Century Thought*. Cambridge, Mass., 1952.

Leavis, F. R. *The Common Pursuit*. London, 1952.

Macdonald, Hugh, ed. *A Journal from Parnassus*. London, 1937.

MacDonald, W. L. *Pope and His Critics: A Study in Eighteenth Century Personalities*. London, 1951.

Mack, Maynard. "On Reading Pope," *College English*, VII (1946), 263–273.

_____. *The Garden and the City: Retirement and Politics in the Later Poetry of Pope, 1731–1743*. Toronto, 1969.

McKillop, Alan D. "Griffith's Pioneer Study of the Progress Piece," in *The Great Torch Race*, ed. Mary Tom Osborne. Austin, 1961.

Marshall, Robert Carlisle. "Aesthetic Aspects of Pope's *Dunciad*," Ph.D. dissertation, University of Texas, 1963.

Panofsky, Erwin. *Studies in Iconology: Humanistic Themes in the Art of the Renaissance*. Oxford, 1939.

Pope, Alexander. *The Art of Sinking in Poetry*, ed. Edna L. Steeves. New York, 1952.

_____. *The Correspondence of Alexander Pope*, ed. George Sherburn. 5 vols. Oxford, 1956.

_____. *The Poems of Alexander Pope*, ed. John Butt et al. 10 vols. London, 1939–1967.

Poetry of Pope's *Dunciad*

_____ et al. *The Memoirs of Martinus Scriblerus,* ed. Charles Kerby-Miller. New Haven, 1950.

Rosenberg, Albert. *Sir Richard Blackmore.* Lincoln, Neb., 1953.

Ruffhead, Owen. *Life of Alexander Pope, Esq.* London, 1769.

Sampson, R. V. *Progress in the Age of Reason: The Seventeenth Century to the Present Day.* London, 1956.

Senault, J. F. *The Use of the Passions,* trans. Henry Carey, Earl of Monmouth. London, 1649.

Sherburn, George. "The *Dunciad,* Book IV," *University of Texas Studies in English,* XXIV (1944), 174–190.

Spence, Joseph. *Observations, Anecdotes, and Characters of Books and Men,* ed. James Osborne. 2 vols. Oxford, 1966.

Spenser, Edmund. *The Works of Edmund Spenser: A Variorum Edition,* ed. Edwin Greenlaw, Charles Grosvenor Osgood, and Frederick Morgan Padelford. 10 vols. Baltimore, 1932–1949.

Swayne, Mattie. "The Progress Piece in the Seventeenth Century," *University of Texas Studies in English,* XVI (1936), 84–92.

Swedenberg, H. T., Jr. *The Theory of the Epic in England, 1650–1800.* University of California Publications in English, Vol. XV. Berkeley, 1944.

Swift, Jonathan. *The Correspondence of Jonathan Swift,* ed. Harold Williams. Oxford, 1963–1965.

Tanner, Tony. "Reason and the Grotesque: Pope's *Dunciad,*" *Critical Quarterly,* VII (1965), 145–160.

Teggart, Frederick J., ed. *The Idea of Progress: A Collection of Readings.* Berkeley and Los Angeles, 1949.

Temple, Sir William. *Five Miscellaneous Essays,* ed. Samuel Holt Monk. Ann Arbor, 1963.

Tillotson, Geoffrey. *On the Poetry of Pope,* 2nd ed. Oxford, 1950.

Warren, Austin. *Alexander Pope as Critic and Humanist.* Princeton, 1929.

Wellek, René. *The Rise of English Literary History.* Chapel Hill, 1941.

Williams, Aubrey L. "Literary Backgrounds to Book Four of the *Dunciad,*" *PMLA,* LXVIII (1953), 806–813.

_____. *Pope's "Dunciad": A Study of Its Meaning.* Baton Rouge and London, 1955.

Wilmot, John, Earl of Rochester. *Poems,* ed. Vivian de Sola Pinto. 2nd ed. Cambridge, Mass., 1964.

Young, Edward. *The Complete Works,* ed. James Nichols. 2 vols. London, 1854.

INDEX

Index

135